Hope Is Here!

Moving Forward on Solid Ground

Clay NeSmith

Sermon To Book
www.sermontobook.com

Hope Is Here! / Clay NeSmith
ISBN-13: 978-1-945793-05-9
ISBN-10: 1-945793-05-8

To my wife Kim, my son Cole, my Church family, and the team of people who helped this book take shape. Y'all are flippin' incredible.

CONTENTS

Note from the Author

Thank you for purchasing *Hope Is Here: Moving Forward on Solid Ground!*

Accompanying each main chapter of the book is a set of reflective questions concluding with an application-oriented action step. These workbook sections are intended to help you recognize your identity in Christ, experience God's freely offered provision for your life, and move through your daily life in hope and faith.

I recommend you go through these workbook sections with a pen in order to write your thoughts and record notes in the areas provided. The questions are suitable for independent reflection, but you could also discuss them with a friend or study group.

Regardless of your reason for picking up this book, I pray that reading it will equip you to move forward victoriously, claiming your God-centered identity and purpose—and then in turn showing others the way of hope.

—*Clay NeSmith*

INTRODUCTION

What Is Hope?

Hope is something that everyone has. All of us hope for something. Some of us hope for a happy life, some people hope for health, and others put their hope in wealth or material possessions. In reality, these things can fail us; what we want to happen might not come to pass. The hope that fails is merely wishful thinking; it is not coupled with faith. It is inevitable that some of our wishful hopes will not be fulfilled—we have an appointment with disappointment!

There is only one in whom we can place our hope and not be disappointed. This hope is concrete. It is a hope we can bank our lives on. The only hope that comes with the assurance of fulfillment is hope in Jesus Christ. This hope is fulfilled because Jesus is here! He promised never to leave us. He is constantly present among us. Jesus comes into our own specific situations and circumstances. He came to Earth in the flesh, remains with us in Spirit, and will come again in His glorified body. Our hope in Christ centers on His future arrival.

When we put all of our trust, faith, and hope into this one promise, we will not be disappointed. Jesus is coming again!

Hope is a motivator. When you have hope in something, you are motivated toward that thing. If you hope for health, you will be motivated to live a healthy lifestyle. If you hope for financial security, your decisions will be guided by the desire to conserve your wealth. You will be motivated to make smart financial choices. Hope motivates us to learn and excites our interest. It can be a beautiful thing, but hope will only remain beautiful when it is mixed with faith.

Faith is what makes hope explode and erupt in our lives. It is what *activates* hope. When coupled with faith, hope produces life in us. We see results. We see change. Life rises up inside of us and inspires us. We will begin to inspire others as this hope works in and through our lives.

Our inspiration comes from the life of Jesus. All of us were born into sin, and were once at enmity with God (Romans 5:12; 8:7). We know that in His death, Christ effectually erased the sin of the world. What, then, will Jesus do when He comes again? What is His purpose in returning? He will not come to take away sin *again*—He has already successfully accomplished that! Jesus will come again to save each one who eagerly awaits His return. Hebrews tells us that "Christ was offered *once for all time* as a sacrifice to take away the sins of many people. He will come again, not to deal with our sins, but to bring salvation to all who are eagerly waiting for him" (Hebrews 9:28 New Living Translation, emphasis added). Who is eagerly waiting for Him? Are you excited for the return of Jesus?

As followers of Christ, we believe in the death, burial, and resurrection of Jesus. We hope in Him because of what He has done and what He is going to do. We have hope because He has already paid for our sins. He has given us a new life. He has given us the means to walk in righteousness, rather than be enslaved to sin (Romans 8:4). We are forgiven. When Jesus comes again, He will receive those who are looking for Him. Are we truly *looking* for His return? Are we ready for Jesus to come back?

We should be excited, anticipating the return of Jesus. Each day holds the potential to be the most amazing day in history. Jesus could come back today. Let's seek to live in that light. Let's not lose sight of His promise. Let's live in a place of expectation and longing for His return. Let us place all of our hope in Jesus!

CHAPTER ONE

Hope Is Here—Not There

On Christmas Day, I woke up at about three o'clock in the morning. Our church had just experienced the amazing conversions of 410 people on Christmas Eve. My soul was alive and refreshed with the goodness of God. When I woke up, God spoke three words to my heart: encourage, motivate, and hope. These are three words that God wanted to birth in the church for the New Year. Encourage. Motivate. Hope.

Just as God was speaking those words into my heart, I got up and was led to a particular passage in His Word. God often works like this—when He speaks something to your spirit, He will usually authenticate it with His written Word. Many people *think* they hear the voice of God, but it needs to be backed up with His Word. God will not contradict Himself by speaking something that goes against all that He has previously revealed to us.

On Christmas Day, God backed up the three words with Scripture. He told me, "Those three words are found in a particular passage in Scripture." God brought me here:

> *Let us hold tightly without wavering to the **hope** we affirm, for God can be trusted to keep his promise. Let us think of ways to **motivate** one another to acts of love and good works. And let us not neglect meeting together, as some people do, but **encourage** one another, especially now that the day of his return is drawing near.* — **Hebrews 10:23-25 NLT (emphasis added)**

The author of Hebrews is writing to those believers who had put their hope in Jesus, but were seeking to return to their old ways. This passage was written to encourage them to live out their full potential in God. Living out our God-potential is about embracing who Jesus is and walking in the fullness of God. It is about moving forward with the hope that God has placed inside of us.

Don't Stay There

That hope is *here*—so we don't have to stay *there*. Where is there? *There* is a different place for every single one of us. It represents the disappointments, the frustrations, and the failures we choose to linger in. It is a stagnant place of the flesh that lures us in with its familiarity. People get stuck *there* because they are accustomed to operating according to the flesh. It's easy to stay there. It's easy to be upset and angry. It's easy to blame someone or something. It's easy to retreat to the past instead of choosing to move forward into the unknown. But when we take the easy way out, we're cut off from progress.

God is about progress. If we want to move forward, we must understand this. He is a moving God. He will never leave you *there* because He knows the place to which you are called. He sees your true potential. There is hope! God is always willing, but we have to cooperate with Him. His will becomes reality when we embrace the hope that He has spoken into our lives. Hope will rise up within us to inspire us to achieve great things for God. Hope is here. We can move forward. Your God-potential is waiting for you to rise.

Hope motivates us to rise; faith inspires us to move forward. Advancement comes by partnering faith with the hope that God has placed in front of us. The Bible says that God has created us for incredible potential (Ephesians 3:20). We can walk into this potential. We can live with purpose and destiny. We don't have to stay *there* or go back to where we used to be, because hope is here.

Just as nurturing hope in our lives inspires us to progress, a lack of hope leads to a withering away. It initiates an opposite, negative cycle. Despair grows where hope is lacking. The soul becomes downcast. It can feel as though our life is being sucked out of us. This will bring us into doubt. Doubt in turn produces dullness, and dullness causes us to despise. Some people have high hopes for their life, but then something creeps in and knocks them down. They never get back up because their hope is shattered. They are living *there*—in the despair, in the failure. As time goes by, they become hardened to their previous hope. They think, "I was so naïve. Why did I think that would work? Who am I? I can't do that. I can't be this." They close themselves off from the hope they once held so close. They begin to despise hope and seek to crush it in other people. They claim to have wisdom by extinguishing the hope and potential they see in other people.

God challenges this trajectory. God wants to give you hope. He does not want you to miss anything. There is something great inside of you waiting to be released. God wants you to move forward; He doesn't want you to stay *there*.

Throughout the Bible, we have examples of God trying to bring out the potential in His people. God always aims to take people to the next level. The Israelites are a great example. They represent us—a nation of people set apart for God. God freed them from captivity, bondage, and slavery. Then He promised to lead them to a place overflowing with life. The Bible calls it the Promised Land, a place flowing with milk and honey. It was a land of great provision (Exodus 3:8). God wanted to move the people of Israel from where they were to where they could be. In the middle of this transition, many of them wanted to go back to where they came from (Exodus 16:3). God was inspiring and motivating the Israelites, but the majority of them decided that they would rather go back to Egypt. They preferred the life of a slave to a life given over to trusting in God.

Does this sound familiar? This is the person who wants to retreat, the person who wants to go back to old ways. The grumbling Israelites ended up missing out on the greatness that God had in store for them (Numbers 26:65). Like them, we might miss out on the goodness God wants to show us if we want to go back to how we used to be.

It's easy to go back. It's exactly what the Israelites wanted. It's exactly what the believers addressed in the book of Hebrews wanted to do (Hebrews 5:12). They wanted to return to the old systems that Christ came to replace. They wanted to go back to sacrificing animals instead of embracing life in the Spirit. The author reminded them that they didn't have to go back to where they came from, because hope had already come! They were free to live out their God-potential. God is saying the same thing to us. We don't have to go back, because we have been set free. We have God-potential. We can accomplish amazing things: "For we are God's masterpiece. He has created us anew in Christ Jesus, so we can do the good things he planned for us long ago" (Ephesians 2:10 NLT). *Hope is here!*

Take God at His Word

In spite of our God-potential, we humans don't always do what we say we will, right? Your spouse may make a promise and then forget about it. Your employer may lack appreciation for your work and prolong a promise of higher pay. People will fail us from time to time, no matter how close they are to us. We will be disappointed by family, friends, coworkers, neighbors— it's inevitable. Some of us live in disappointment with our spouses. Maybe they don't say the right things. Maybe they don't truly understand us. We, in turn, disappoint others. We withhold love. We aren't always attentive to the needs of those around us.

God is not like us. He does not fail us. God will do what He says He will do. Believe this. Every promise of God will come to pass. When we embrace this truth, hope begins to rise up. The Bible says, "Let us hold tightly without wavering to the hope we affirm, for God can be trusted to keep his promise" (Hebrews 10:23 NLT). God can be trusted!

Jesus made a promise on the cross that we often fail to comprehend. He said, "It is finished!" (John 19:30). His work was declared complete. His purpose was to take away the sin of the world (John 1:29). Jesus was referring to *our* sin. It is finished; our sins are gone. They are paid in full. This should encourage and motivate us! All of your sins have been paid for. It is finished—it is over. You are forgiven!

Unfortunately, many people don't believe in this finished work of Christ. They might proclaim it with their mouths, but they lack a revelation of the finality of God's forgiveness. They do not understand that the work of Christ was completed two thousand years ago. They live fruitless lives, devoid of understanding and hope. They live under condemnation, believing that if they screw up, Jesus will leave them.

God's Word utterly destroys this mentality. The Bible says that God will never leave you nor forsake you (Deuteronomy 31:8; Hebrews 13:5). As a matter of fact, Jesus said something amazing: "I am with you always,

even to the end of the age" (Matthew 28:20 NLT).
Always! All the time, forever! The Presence of God in
our lives is a promise. Jesus told us Himself. His
Presence is determined by Him alone. He will be with us
always—no matter where we may find ourselves. Many
of us have a hard time embracing this truth, but the
simple reality is that if you trust in Jesus, there's nothing
you can do to thwart His plan. He will always be with
you. It is finished. The Bible says He paid for it (1
Timothy 2:6). We didn't pay for it; we didn't work for it.
It's not dependent on what we do: The only thing that
matters is what He's already done. He made a promise.
He said, "It is finished!" (John 19:30). It is over, paid in
full. All your misses—those in the past, and those in the
future—are already paid for. This gives me hope, and it
should give you hope, too.

It doesn't depend on us. We have freedom to live in
hope and confidence. Even if we mess up, we can still
have hope, because our hope rests in His completed
work. This allows us to move past mistakes and press
forward into our potential. We must trust what Christ has
done on the cross. We are forgiven.

There is a verse that says, "For [God's] anger lasts
only a moment..." (Psalm 30:5 NLT). That moment was
taken out on the cross. His anger was fully satisfied. The
next part of the verse continues: "...but his favor lasts a
lifetime! Weeping may last through the night, but joy
comes with the morning" (Psalm 30:5 NLT).

Many people wish for the favor of God in their lives.
The Bible tells us that the favor of God is already
present. His favor is on you right now. He wants to see

you fulfill your potential, because He sees more in you than you see in yourself. Forgiveness has happened, but favor is yours to embrace. And this favor will last your entire lifetime!

The Lie of the Enemy

The enemy wants us to get these things backward. He wants us to doubt God's Word and believe that forgiveness and favor only last for a second. The enemy wants us to be sidetracked with a lie and miss out on our full potential.

Hope is here, but we can become blinded to that hope when we buy into the deception of the enemy. He wants us to think that we have to try more, that we have to strive to free ourselves of oppression. Remember that Jesus revealed to us the purpose of the enemy, which is to oppress you and hold you back from inheriting all that God has promised you, all that God has *already* provided.

The enemy tells us that we need to provide for ourselves. He says that we're not good enough, that we've got to earn more. He tells us to work harder to earn God's favor, to get baptized again, to memorize more Scripture, to spend more time in prayer. These are good things, but when they come from the mouth of the enemy, they are riddled with guilt, insecurity, fear, and hopelessness. He tries to get you caught up in the systems and practices so that you try to make provisions for yourself, instead of receiving God's provision.

The enemy is like a crooked mortgage lender. Let's say you go to buy a new house and you put a thirty-year mortgage on it, making monthly payments. You set up these monthly installments for thirty years, but shortly after you put the down payment on the house, a good friend comes and pays the house off in full to the banker! That friend came in and paid the entire mortgage, but that crooked banker continues to take monthly installments from you for the next thirty years. He didn't tell you that someone came in and paid it in full. He continued to let you worry and stress about how you were going to make the payments, and even threatened to foreclose on you should you fail to meet the deadlines. This is how the enemy operates.

Many people today are continually buying into the lies of the enemy. They continue to make "monthly payments" for their sin, not realizing that they have a King who already paid every penny!

The enemy wants to steal your focus, your future, and the favor of God upon your life. He wants you to continually question what God has already revealed. He wants you to underestimate the Word of God. The Bible tells us that He is with us, but then someone gets a flat tire and says, "Where is God in this? God must not be with me because I cussed at my wife before I left for work." We question God's forgiveness. We make mistakes and think forgiveness must be won all over again. God's Word says that Jesus died once for sin. If you stop focusing on the sin and instead focus on your future, you will be set free to do the amazing things that God has called you to do.

The enemy tries to hide the truth from us—the truth that we are God's glorious inheritance, that God has made a provision for us, and that we can bank our lives on this hope.

The Israelites experienced God's provision in the face of their enemy. When Pharaoh refused to set them free from slavery, God unleashed ten plagues on Egypt. The tenth plague that finally softened the stubborn heart of Pharaoh was the death of every firstborn throughout the land of Egypt, but God made a provision for the Israelites. He told each family to kill a lamb and put its blood over their doorpost. The angel of death would bypass any home with the blood painted on the doorpost; however, God would strike every household that didn't make this provision.

The Bible tells us that it was a night of crying and wailing throughout the land of Egypt (Exodus 12:30). Every house in the land that failed to apply the blood of the lamb had death visited upon them—but every household that allowed God's provision was spared. The enemy wants to hold us back and keep us in Egypt, but God has made a provision for us to set us free from the enemy—the shed blood of Jesus on the cross! The sacrifice has been made once and for all. It is finished. The enemy has no power over those who put their hope in God's provision.

People get this mixed up. They spend their lives doing religious exercises and miss the favor of God because they are constantly trying to be forgiven. I'm talking about churched people, believers who should know better. It is finished! It is over! It is paid in full! You don't have to earn it. Jesus did it for you. Take the focus off your sin and put it on the favor of God. You are the child of the King. Learn this and you will be propelled into the great future He has in store for you.

What hinders us is our desire to get better, to do better, to be better. It causes us to emphasize the wrong things. I used to think, "I want to build this church." Preachers do that all the time. They want to build up the Church; they want to do greater things. God quickly reminds me that *He* will build His church. He will do what He says He will do. He says He will build His Church if you will have audacious faith like Peter had. He says, "I will build my church..." (Matthew 16:18). But if your focus centers on "Shoot, *I've* got to build the church," then you open the door for the enemy to steal the favor from your life.

Too many of us are trying to do better in our own power. We focus on fixing the problem, but in doing so we miss out on the solution. If you want a better marriage, focusing on a having a better marriage will have an adverse effect. In our own effort, we try and try and try. And then when we fail, disappointment sets in because we have been focused on the wrong thing. If you choose to focus on what Christ has done and what Christ has said, then your marriage will get better. We need to conquer this addiction of trying to solve things by our own power. We need to shift our focus. But how in the world do we do that?

We set our focus on God by putting Him and His Word first. After all, hope is here because of what God's

Word says. You can be motivated to let God's gifts inside of you come alive and change the world.

The truth is that the favor of God rests upon your life and you are the child of a King. This is an inspiring revelation. You can walk in the fullness of whom God says you are. Don't buy into the lie of the enemy and try to pay for something that has already been paid for. This will immobilize you and cause you to ask for more and more from a God who has already given you all things. You are not waiting for God; He is waiting for you.

As you continually meet with other people, you will be encouraged on your journey. I'm inviting you to embrace hope. You belong to the king of kings, the same One who was resurrected from the dead, and you can walk in the fullness of the favor He has lavished upon you. You do not have to go back to where you came from. You do not have to stay where you are. You can move forward because hope is here.

Store Up Hope

It is true that Christ is here and consequently hope is here, but realize that everything else is here, too. Challenges are here. Accidents are here. Mistakes are here. Mishaps and bad relationships are here. Hope is here, but some days are tough. We still become satisfied and distracted by false hopes. How do we begin to really store up concrete hope so that we walk by faith and live in the promises of God?

Jesus warned us of the enemy who comes to steal, kill, and destroy, and who tries to rob us of God's promises, but then He reveals His own purpose, which is to give us "a rich and satisfying life" (John 10:10). He gives us a life of great abundance, a life overflowing with every spiritual blessing, a life of plenty. There is a very real enemy on Earth who seeks to deceive you. But Jesus came to offset the power, influence, and intentions of that enemy. In the midst of the struggle, He has come to give us life to the fullest. He allows us to store up hope.

Exodus records the story of the Israelites in Egypt. The Israelites were under bondage, slavery, and oppression for four hundred years in Egypt. They were crying out to God because of their suffering. They were a hopeless people, clutched in the iron grip of Pharaoh. When they cried out to God, He heard their cry. God appointed a man named Moses to demand freedom for the Israelites. Out of the stubbornness of his heart, Pharaoh resisted Moses many times. The enemy would not let God's people go, so God made a provision for them. He made the great promise to them that He would move them from a land of oppression to a land of plenty. He led them to the Promised Land, "a land flowing with milk and honey" (Exodus 3:17). As they trusted in their creator, He provided for them. God's provision to the Israelites was a foreshadowing of what was to come in Christ.

Jesus does the same thing for us in the New Testament. He tells the enemy, "Let my people go!" He makes a provision for us, because sin and the deception of the enemy hold us captive. Jesus shed His blood to fulfill His promise. He paid a high price to set us free to live as sons and daughters of the King (Galatians 5:1). As we trust in Jesus, He provides for us.

In order to store up our hope, we have to trust in God's provision. We have to activate our faith in the concrete hope of Jesus Christ. Faith leads us to the promise. Hope gives faith something to aim for. My prayer is that we as God's people will store up our hope to activate and strengthen the faith in our lives. Then we will begin to inherit the great promises of God. A life devoid of hope will stop faith dead in its tracks. We have to claim our inheritance. We have to store up our hope in Jesus. And by faith, we will begin to take ground.

Paul tells us in Ephesians:

> *I pray that your hearts will be flooded with light so that you can understand the **confident** hope he has given to those he called—his holy people who are his rich and **glorious inheritance.***
>
> *I also pray that you will understand the incredible greatness of God's power for us who believe him. This is the same mighty power that raised Christ from the dead and seated him in the place of honor at God's right hand in the heavenly realms. — **Ephesians 1:18-20 NLT (emphasis added)***

Paul tells us that *we* are God's glorious inheritance! We can have solid hope, concrete hope, *confident hope*, because we are the inheritance of God Almighty, the creator of the universe. This hope allows us to build up our faith so that we can inherit the promise. Faith will allow us to walk in the "incredible greatness of God's power." The same power that raised Jesus from the dead is available to every single one of us! This is something to hope for.

Shaky Ground

The sad thing is that many of us are missing out on the fullness of God's promises. We lack the assurance that comes with trusting God because we rely on ourselves too much, trying to earn our way to being His children. We need to walk in the confidence of our identities in Christ. We need to stop lingering on shaky ground!

If your life is devoid of vibrant, concrete hope, it's because you are putting your hope into the wrong thing. Since faith is motivated by solid hope, they are interconnected. With no solid hope, nothing will inspire faith in your life. You will lack faith, hope, motivation, and inspiration. You will hop from one shaky ground to the next, constantly struggling to fill the gaps in your life.

Shaky ground manifests in all areas of life and in many different ways. Today it is common for people to put their hope into their relationships. While relationships themselves are blessings from God, they are no substitute for the unfailing love, acceptance, and endless source of hope found in Jesus. When one relationship gives way, causes disappointment, or brings frustration, we hop to the next one, hoping that it will be better. We blame others in the process. Bitterness takes root. A false sense of hope compels us to move on and continue to desperately search for fulfillment elsewhere.

Others may hop from church to church, job to job, bed to bed. They are never satisfied. The desire to find solid ground dominates their lives. They don't run toward anything great, because they are too distracted. God's promises aren't fulfilled because they are continually hopping from one thing to another.

The Bible tells us how to find solid ground: "Now faith is *confidence* in what we hope for and *assurance* about what we do not see. This is what the ancients were commended for" (Hebrews 11:1-2 NIV, emphasis added). Confidence and assurance come by faith. Faith brings stability and solid ground.

Another translation puts it this way: "Now faith is the *substance* of things hoped for, the evidence of things not seen. For by it the elders obtained a *good testimony*" (Hebrews 11:1-2 NKJV, emphasis added). Things of substance come through faith, which in turn bring an incredible reputation with the people who surround you. They will notice that you are walking on solid ground. Those who linger on shaky ground will be drawn to you. Your testimony may save their lives.

A Living Testimony

God has revealed His plan to us. He describes the Church not as a building, but as a people called to inherit the riches of His blessings. He has shown us the true purpose of the Church. In His Word, Paul tells us:

And this is God's plan: Both Gentiles and Jews who believe the Good News share equally in the riches inherited by

God's children. Both are part of the same body, and both enjoy the promise of blessings because they belong to Christ Jesus. By God's grace and mighty power, I have been given the privilege of serving him by spreading this Good News.

Though I am the least deserving of all God's people, he graciously gave me the privilege of telling the Gentiles about the endless treasures available to them in Christ. I was chosen to explain to everyone this mysterious plan that God, the Creator of all things, had kept secret from the beginning.

*God's purpose in all this was **to use the church to display his wisdom** in its rich variety **to all the unseen rulers and authorities in the heavenly places.** This was his eternal plan, which he carried out through Christ Jesus our Lord. — **Ephesians 3:6-11 NLT (emphasis added)***

God's purpose for the Church—for all those who believe in the Good News of Jesus Christ—is to display the wisdom of God. We are living testimonies to both those around us and especially to "unseen rulers and authorities in the heavenly places." We are on display, not just to our neighbors, kids, and coworkers, but to the powers and principalities in the spiritual dimensions of the universe. You are teaching the angels and demons something about God!

Hope is here, God has a plan, and you have a challenge—but the challenge doesn't shatter the promise. When you face trials, understand the plan of the creator. Understand that it's higher than me, it's higher than you, and it's higher than our immediate problems. We are walking in the midst of the spiritual dimension, on display for good and for evil, for angels and for demons, for all the principalities and powers of the universe. We are standing in the middle of the arena as we face life's difficulties. We have the opportunity to display the wisdom of God to all of creation!

That's a powerful plan. I love my wife dearly, but I understand that I'm not a display for her. I'm not a display for you. I'm a display for God to an audience in the spiritual realm. Sometimes we are hindered by our challenges because we think they are a result of wrongdoing—that we've screwed up and have to face the consequences. Yet in this, we miss the significance of what is actually happening: we have challenges so that we can show the power of God that is at work in our lives!

We can break this down even further to get a clearer picture. The Bible teaches that we have a very real enemy on Earth: Satan. He once had a high place in heaven, but he decided that he wanted to rise above God and rebelled against Him. The Bible says that God cast him out of heaven, along with one-third of the angels who also chose to rebel against God (Revelation 12:9). They are now relegated to the earthly domain—where we live.

By placing humans in the same realm as Satan, God was challenging him. God knew that Satan would convince humans to fall into sin and turn against Him, but He also had a plan. He sent a Redeemer who would release humans from the grip and influence of the enemy. Once freed from Satan's tyranny, they would choose to worship God Almighty. They would turn their eyes toward Him, giving Him allegiance, praise, honor,

and glory—in the midst of Satan's own domain!
Through trials, challenges, hard times, and the deceit of
the enemy, they would choose to trust in God!

You are on display. If you are being challenged,
realize that you are standing in the middle of an arena!
Your reaction in the midst of trials will speak volumes to
all the powers and principalities of the universe who are
watching you. If you can wrap your heart and mind
around this incredible plan of God's rich and glorious
love for you, it will change the way you live life. Just
because things aren't going your way, doesn't mean
there isn't a promise in front of you. Whatever tries to
come against you cannot touch what God has already
declared.

The enemy doesn't want you to grasp this truth. He
wants to keep you scared, afraid to step out and believe
God for greater things. He comes at you daily, trying to
influence your mind. You need to wake up each day
realizing that God has a plan. You are a beloved child of
God. Satan's power has already been utterly broken by
the work completed on the cross. God has made a
provision for us, and we can choose to walk in the
fullness of His promise. We can live in whom He says
that we are!

Seek First the Kingdom

The oppression of the enemy has no place in the life
of the believer of Jesus Christ. A provision has been
made. No longer do you have to live under the bondage
of the enemy. Salvation is not a reward for the amazing

good things you have done—it is a free gift from God. The meaning of the gospel is literally "good news." It is good news to realize that it's no longer up to us to free ourselves from bondage.

Then why do we choose to remain in bondage rather than receive the provision that God has made? We have an eternal connection to our creator. It came in the form of Jesus being crucified and then resurrected. Our trust in God to receive this gift is what sets us free, establishes hope, and paves the way for more faith to do greater works.

Paul reminds us in Ephesians:

> *But God is so rich in mercy, and he loved us so much, that even though we were dead because of our sins, he gave us life when he raised Christ from the dead. (It is only by God's grace that you have been saved!) For he raised us from the dead along with Christ and seated us with him in the heavenly realms because we are united with Christ Jesus. So God can point to us in all future ages as examples of the incredible wealth of his grace and kindness toward us, as shown in all he has done for us who are united with Christ Jesus.*
>
> *God saved you by his grace when you believed. And you can't take credit for this; it is a gift from God. Salvation is not a reward for the good things we have done, so none of us can boast about it.* — **Ephesians 2:4-9**

God is rich in His mercy. He gave us more than we bargained for. He salvaged us and freed us from oppression. God points to us as living testimonies of His incredible wealth, grace, and kindness. We are united with Christ Jesus. Our belief and trust in God's provision gives us solid hope. His provision is a gift, and you don't earn gifts—you receive them!

God is only impressed with one thing: your response to the hope He offers. The Bible tells us to shift our focus to God, and then every other problem will fall into place. Jesus said:

> *Therefore do not worry, saying, "What shall we eat?" or "What shall we drink?" or "What shall we wear?" For after all these things the Gentiles seek. For your heavenly Father knows that you need all these things. But seek first the kingdom of God and His righteousness, and all these things shall be added to you"* — **Matthew 6:31-33 (NKJV)**

Will you seek God's Kingdom? Will you live in His blessed assurance? Will you store up your hope and believe? Will you activate your faith and press toward His promise of abundant life? Will you receive His provision? God calls us to put our hope and trust in His provision so that faith will abound in our lives. We will then be activated, inspired, and motivated to receive the full promises of God—and that's really good news!

It's interesting that the word "first" in the passage above was translated from the Greek word *protos*. *Protos* literally means "first in rank, first in order." But it also means "that which everything else revolves around." Everything else revolves around whatever is at the center of your life.

We're hindered when we replace God as the center of our lives. We put our hope and our focus on something else instead of first seeking His Kingdom and His righteousness. Whenever something else besides God becomes the center of our attention, then nothing else in life will go right—even if that center is a "good" thing, like marriage. That's why focusing on solving your marital issues over and above focusing on God doesn't work.

We need to realize who Jesus is, what He's done, and the favor He's lavished upon us. Jesus is telling us that He wants to be the center. And when we make Him the center, we experience life in its fullness. We begin to move forward and progress. Jesus is calling us to move our problems out of the center and put Him in as the central hub—that which everything else revolves around. Your marriage, your finances, your career, and your relationships will all be balanced out—because Jesus is the Source that changes everything else. With Jesus as the center, your life will begin to roll.

Many of us are trying to change circumstances by what we do. We have it backward! It's what *He* has done in our lives. His Spirit partners with us and coaches us into a higher life. God will do what He says He will do. If He paid for sin, then sin is paid for. If He says you've got a brighter future, then you've got a brighter future. But do you take Him at His Word? Do you embrace hope? Do you embrace the truth and take strides in faith toward it?

You aren't embracing hope if you continually put the problem in the center. That's where many people remain today. They just want to get better. Jesus promised us life, abundant life (John 10:10). You don't get better by *trying* more; you get better by *trusting* more. Trusting allows us to walk in the fullness of the very God who speaks life into your spirit. How do we instill hope into our lives? Put Jesus in the center, and trust that God will do what He says He will do.

Chapter 1 Questions

Question: In what places besides God might you be looking for hope? How can you redirect your focus?

_____

_____

_____

_____

_____

_____

_____

_____

_____

_____

_____

_____

Question: For what, exactly, are we to hope in God? What forms the basis for this hope?

_____

_____

_____

_____

_____

_____

_____

_____

_____

_____

_____

_____

Question: What lies has the enemy tried to tell you? How have you responded? What would the best response be (or have been)?

_____

_____

_____

_____

_____

_____

_____

_____

_____

_____

Question: In what areas of your life are you standing on shaky ground? How, specifically, can you firm up that ground?

_____

_____

_____

_____

_____

_____

_____

_____

_____

_____

_____

Question: What specific steps can you take to seek the Kingdom first in your daily life?

_____

_____

_____

_____

_____

_____

_____

_____

_____

_____

_____

Action: Don't stay where you are. Instead of believing the lies of the enemy, immerse yourself in God's Word and take Him at His Word. If you find yourself standing on shaky ground, focus on seeking the Kingdom first and storing up hope in the Lord. Be a living testimony to His grace!

Chapter 1 Notes

CHAPTER TWO

Living Out Our Hope

I was a wannabe golfer at the age of eighteen. Now, I am a frustrated golfer with antique clubs that have been sitting in the garage for twenty years. When I tried the game out as a teenager, I would swing so hard that the ball never went in the intended direction. I could never put the sink the shot. I never even knew which club to use for any particular shot. I would swing and go over the top of the ball, and all I'd hear was wind. Or my club would hit behind the ball, sending dirt flying, and the ball would roll about eight feet.

My friends would laugh at me whenever I would swing and miss the ball. With nobody to encourage me or teach me how to properly play the game, I lost all motivation. I took my clubs and hid them in the back of the garage in a closet—and now they are antiques. I am still very insecure when it comes to the game of golf. If you invited me out to play, I would probably decline, assuming that once you found out how bad I was, you'd make fun of me.

The interesting thing is, the tools needed to sink the shot are the same ones sitting in my garage gathering dust. If I ever want to overcome my failure in this area, I'm going to need those very clubs I rejected. Without knowing it, we do this in other areas of our lives, too. In order to "sink the shot" in life—to experience real satisfaction and joy—there are tools that we need. The problem is that many of us have taken those tools and stuffed them in a closet somewhere in the back of the garage.

Some of us have given up on the game of life—hope has somehow drained away. We're missing so much opportunity, so much joy, so much of the incredible life that God has prepared for us. We overcompensate by trying to move on to something else. We think God has given up on us, so we give up on Him. We think that God is mad at us. We imagine Him as an intimidating God who will laugh at us as our friends did when we missed the shot. We may feel discouraged, ashamed, and guilty. We define ourselves by our mistakes. We've taken our relationship with God and shoved it in the back of the garage somewhere. The tools needed to sink the shot are present, but we lack the understanding of how to properly use those tools.

All of us have missed at something in life. We've missed the mark of God's glorious standard. We've all sinned and fallen short of where God has called us (Romans 3:23). And that can cause deep discouragement unless we embrace the hope found only in Christ.

As we saw in Chapter 1, the problem is that we don't understand who God is. We are confused about how He

works. We misinterpret His plan for our lives. The Bible
tells us that for those in Christ, there is no condemnation
(Romans 8:1). The guilt and shame that you are feeling
does not come from your creator. Your creator is a God
of encouragement, a God who sees more in you than you
see in yourself. If you begin to embrace who He says
that you are instead of who you think you are, you can
get back in the game and experience joy and hope in life.

God has a plan for your life. He has a standard for
your life and He wants to equip you to hit the mark, to
sink the shot. The Bible says:

> *But now God has shown us a way to be made right with
> him without keeping the requirements of the law, as was
> promised in the writings of Moses and the prophets long
> ago. We are made right with God by placing our faith in
> Jesus Christ. And this is true for everyone who believes, no
> matter who we are.* — ***Romans 3:21-22 NLT***

The writings of Moses and the prophets were pointing
toward the way to be made right with God. The systems
and structures point us toward how to be made right with
God—by placing our faith in Jesus Christ, not by
keeping the law.

If you are confused about who God is and you've lost
the sense of hope in your life, my prayer is that God's
Word can instill hope back in you. You may be
discouraged, but I believe you will be encouraged as we
talk about how to hit the mark. God's plan for your life is
to sink the shot—not for you to keep missing, but for

you to hit the mark of His incredible standard, to live out His awesome plan for your life.

Best Ball

For everyone has sinned; we all fall short of God's glorious standard. Yet God, in his grace, freely makes us right in his sight. He did this through Christ Jesus when he freed us from the penalty for our sins. For God presented Jesus as the sacrifice for sin. People are made right with God when they believe that Jesus sacrificed his life, shedding his blood. — Romans 3:23-25 NLT

We all fall short of God's standard—but God in His kindness declares us righteous. People are made right with God when they believe in the sacrifice of Jesus. God gave a gift to the human race. He gave His one and only Son so that our misses could be forgiven. Doing life with Jesus is similar to playing the game of golf. We allow His Spirit to coach us to help us sink the shot.

There is a game in golf called "Best Ball." No matter what kind of shot you hit, everyone takes their ball and moves it to wherever the best shot landed. When played with a group of skilled golfers, you can be confident that however horribly you might mess up, all that distance will be covered by someone in the group with a good shot. You are guaranteed to make up all the distance you missed.

That's who Jesus is—He makes up all the distance in the world for every one of our misses, whether they are past, present, or future. All your sin has been forgiven. That means He provides a way for you to take your ball and move it to where His ball is. He is the perfect sacrifice and He hits the ball just right every time.

Coached to Greatness

Jesus makes up all the distance in the world. He forgives us of all our misses. But if all He did was hit the shot perfectly and never teach you how to hit, He would be a terrible coach. Too many Christians have received forgiveness, but remain frustrated. They're like unskilled golfers playing Best Ball, with no knowledge of how to improve.

I want Jesus to forgive me and make up all the distance in my life, but I also want to learn how to get to where He is. I want to learn how to hit a good shot. I want to do something incredible with my life. I don't want to just be forgiven. I want to be coached to greatness.

We often miss out on the vastness of God, the fullness of who He is. God didn't just give us favor to forgive us. God gives us favor so we can accomplish something great for Him in life. He forgave you, yes—but He also desires to coach you. Our heavenly Father, our great God, the creator of the universe, is also an incredible coach!

A great coach doesn't just forgive you for making a mistake, but will teach you how to get it right so that you can hit on all cylinders and play the game well. That's who God is.

Imagine we were practicing archery, and you just kept missing the target. You hit all the trees around the target—and I still didn't get mad at you. In fact, I told you it was okay, to keep trying. But even though I had the knowledge to teach you how to properly aim and fire, I never shared any advice with you. I withheld the vital information that could improve your accuracy. In this scenario, I wouldn't be a very good coach. Actually, I wouldn't even be coaching at all—I'd just be encouraging your failure.

It's the same with God. He not only shows us that He forgive us, but He also equips us with the knowledge and tools necessary to hit the mark. First, He forgives us for missing the mark, and then He teaches us, by His grace, how to sink the shot.

Jesus has made up all the distance in the world; He has forgiven our misses. But you see, grace is so much more than just forgiveness. Grace is forgiveness with a great future. Grace is unmerited favor. It's undeserved and unearned. God forgives you, but He also continually teaches you—if you will receive it from Him.

Grace has a name: Jesus. He came to forgive you and coach you to greatness. The Bible tells us:

For the grace of God has been revealed, bringing salvation to all people. And we are instructed to turn from godless living and sinful pleasures. We should live in this evil world with wisdom, righteousness, and devotion to God, while we look forward with hope to that wonderful day when the glory of our great God and Savior, Jesus Christ, will be revealed. He gave his life to free us from every kind of sin, to cleanse us, and to make us his very own people, totally committed to doing good deeds. —**Titus 2:11-14 NLT**

God's grace is Jesus, God in the flesh. Not only does grace bring us salvation, but it instructs us and teaches us. It invites us to live in the way of righteousness. God is not a God who forgives us and then forgets about us. This is why so many of us are frustrated in life—because we believe God forgives us and then just moves on and forgets us. God remembers you and He coaches you. He cares about you and He has a great plan for you. His plan is to give you a future (Jeremiah 29:11). It's a plan to deposit something in you so that you can live out your God-potential. Grace has a future—if you'll learn to walk in the rhythms of grace and learn how to take the shots.

Don't be afraid to pick up your antique clubs again. Maybe you've put God in the corner of your garage. Maybe God seems like an antique to you, some far-off figure with a fuzzy beard, pointing at you and waiting for you to screw up. *But that is not who God is.* God does not come with an accusing finger. We already know who the accuser is. Jesus didn't come into the world to condemn the world (John 3:17). Rather, He came into the world with arms wide open to receive us, make His home inside of us, and coach us to incredible greatness.

We can make no progress at all if we fail to understand that *we are accepted.* That's the foundation—having absolute confidence that nothing can compromise God's love and acceptance.

In order to learn how to sink the shot, there are three principles we need to learn to live by.

Loosen Up

Once we understand that we are accepted, then we can *loosen up*. We can quit trying to earn acceptance. We can stop trying to pay a debt that's already been paid. Jesus came to fulfill what the law was pointing toward. He only tells us to trust Him and walk with Him—and He will help us become all that we were created to be.

Now I know we often look at each other and say, "You better tighten up or God's going to punish you! You better clean up your act quick!" That's what we like to say, right? But Jesus is saying, "Would you loosen up? I've come to make up all the distance in the world." God will coach you in how to loosen up.

Being tense can cause us to miss opportunities. In the game of golf, if you're tightened up, you'll miss the shot. A good instructor will teach you not to over-grip the club. You have to be loose to properly hit the ball. Stress works against this—you can't remain loose while you're stressed out. Stress will make you play at your worst.

The scenario may play out like this: You miss your first shot. People begin to laugh and you start to tense up. If missing wasn't bad enough, you now have the fear of man creeping up on you. You want to impress your friends, so you swing for the fences. The powerful swing coupled with stress is not a good combination. The shot spirals out of control. Stress brings on more stress. Everything goes downhill from there. But if you would just loosen up your grip a little bit, things would go smoother. Relaxation makes a big difference.

Don't focus on the mechanics. I was talking to a pro golfer one time. She said the interesting thing about a golf swing is that it has to have both the right structure and the right motion. When the structure and the motion work together, it causes this incredible movement. She told me, "If we have motion without structure, we will be all over the place. But structure without motion never really accomplishes anything."

The interesting thing is that God gave us structure a long time ago. That structure was the law, the regulations that the Jewish people lived under. That law, that structure, was to point them toward the One who would open up the door for them to have full access to God. His name was Jesus.

The problem is that people start to focus on the structure itself, instead of the One who fulfilled that structure. When Jesus came in the flesh, walking among the people, they missed the very thing that could have caused movement in their lives. They were so focused on whether they were doing the right thing or not that they overlooked the One who established the structure of the law in the first place! They had the structure but lacked the motion.

Many Christians today are preoccupied with the mechanics. They ask all the wrong questions: "What am I allowed to do? What should I stay away from? Will God punish me for this? How can I gain God's blessing?" They try to produce all the answers themselves, instead of living and walking with the one True Solution. If we learn to walk with God in the rhythms of grace Jesus offers us, that movement will become natural. Things will begin to happen, but first we need to loosen up.

Christians may even miss the underlying meaning of some Church practices. For instance, let's examine the symbolism of the Lord's Supper. Jesus came to give His life on a cross. He shed His blood to give you full access to God. He sacrificed His body. It is a new day. There is a new covenant, a covenant of grace. At the Last Supper, Jesus tells His disciples to eat the bread and drink the cup in remembrance of Him (1 Corinthians 11:23-26). Every time we take it, we remember the One who opened up our way to God, and empowered us to walk in righteousness.

This significance will bypass us if we're worried about the mechanics. Instead of remembering Jesus and the joy He brings us, people may be thinking: "Did I sip the cup right? Did I do it in the right context? Do I drink juice or do I drink wine? Do I eat unleavened bread? Is this cracker really part of Jesus's body?" We can get distracted by all this stuff and miss the very meaning of the practice. It's not the mechanics that make us right with God; it's the One who the mechanics point us toward.

When we get caught up in systems and structures, we miss out. We don't enjoy life because we are over-gripping the club. We're uptight about what we can and can't do. The Bible says that what makes you right with God is the finished work on the cross. We do follow biblical principles and practices, but for the purpose of guiding us toward the One who brings abundant life.

Loosen up, and begin to focus on the One who came to make you right with God. He has already fully accepted you. You can stop trying to prove yourself, and instead you can walk in unforced rhythms of grace. You are the child of the King. You are a prince. You are a princess. This is based on who Jesus is and what He did for us. Jesus did it, not you. It's by grace alone. Simply believe.

Rest in Jesus. Jesus tells us, "Come to me, all of you who are weary and carry heavy burdens, and I will give you rest. Take my yoke upon you. Let me teach you, because I am humble and gentle at heart, and you will find rest for your souls. For my yoke is easy to bear, and the burden I give you is light" (Matthew 11:28-30 NLT). He came to take weight off of you, not to put more weight on you. Loosen your grip on your performance and tighten up your hope in Jesus.

Maybe you are uptight and thinking about how you failed again today. Loosen up. You've been forgiven if you've believed in Jesus. It's a forgiveness that He offers, not one that you deserve. And because He promised it, it's as good as done. He says, "Rest! Rest in who I say you are."

Before he was stoned to death, Stephen called the Jewish leaders at the high council "stiff-necked" (Acts 7:51 NKJV). He wasn't being mean; he was pointing out that they were stiff instead of loose. They didn't know how to receive grace or trust in Jesus, and they resisted the leading of the Holy Spirit. It's interesting because dancing involves loosening up. You can't force the moves; you follow the rhythm. People who are too tight can't dance with grace. Jesus calls us to move along with the One who created the moves. When we do this, God starts to do amazing things in our lives.

You will continue to miss as long as you keep trying to force it yourself; but if you learn from the One who can help you swing, He will take the weight off. You have full access to God and the ability to learn how to do life. He forgives you and desires to coach you to greatness.

This is the beginning of the journey to put the ball in the hole and sink the shot. You're totally accepted and highly valued by God. Jesus came and did work on the cross that we couldn't do ourselves. You couldn't earn it even if you tried to. Jesus came to do the work for you. He only asks you to trust in Him.

Listen Up

Not only do we need to loosen up, but we also need to *listen up.* If you want to succeed, listen to what God says. He is an incredible teacher. He will help you hit a hole-in-one. He will help you sink the shot.

God teaches us through His Word that equips us to do great things in life. It is holistic. It is an inspired, timeless truth that applies to every area of our lives. It will help you in your marriage. It will guide you in using your money and resources. It will influence your relationships. His Word coaches you to greatness. God is for you, not against you. He wants you to succeed. He wants you to live life to its fullest. If we listen to Him,

He will teach us how to do life. He will show us which club to pull out of the bag for each shot.

Don't use the wrong club. We become frustrated with life because we don't know which club to pull out of the bag. Maybe we've never really sought God in His Word to discover how to hit the shot. Maybe we misuse the club, or misinterpret the shot. Many people don't know which truth to use in a given circumstance, so they try to use the wrong club. When it doesn't work, they start to question God. They think God isn't who He says He is. They lose hope.

Let's look at a concrete example. The Bible says to have a great marriage, so I pull out the "club" of marriage. I examine Scripture to figure out how to make my marriage work. The Bible says, "wives should submit to your husbands in everything" (Ephesians 5:24 NLT). I conclude that in order to have a great marriage with my wife, she needs to be submissive to me. So I try to force it. I say, "Here's the club. Now she needs to submit."

But I've misinterpreted it. I told her she needs to be submissive, and I've swung the club—but my marriage is still on the rocks because she is not being submissive. I missed the second part of the passage: "...husbands, this means love your wives, just as Christ loved the church" (Ephesians 5:25 NLT). I misused the Word of God, and I wondered why God's Word didn't work in that area of my life. I pulled out the wrong club.

The game of golf is like the game of life. There are numerous holes—various facets and challenges—in your life. To succeed, you need to pull out the right club for

each specific scenario. Too often we pull the right club
out on one hole and the wrong one on another. We'll get
a hole-in-one in our marriage, but we won't pull out the
right club in our finances. And then we wonder why God
seems to be failing us.

God's way is best. Another common mistake we
make is that we think we know better than God. We read
and understand the Scripture, but then we start to
overthink it and question it. We pull out the club that
God tells us to use and say, "This doesn't seem like it
will work. This swing doesn't feel right. I'm going to do
it my own way." Then we fail and blame it on God. The
good news is that God has already forgiven us. He is
always waiting with open arms for us to turn back to
Him. If you are tired of doing it your way, try it His way
and be coached to success!

Along the journey, it doesn't always feel good—but
the results are guaranteed to work for your benefit. We
must learn to follow His way. If you are willing to
receive the good news and the coaching of greatness in
your life, it is available! Do you trust your creator?

In the Bible, Paul tells Timothy:

*You have been taught the holy Scriptures from childhood,
and they have given you the wisdom to receive the
salvation that comes by trusting in Christ Jesus. All
Scripture is inspired by God and is useful to teach us what
is true and to make us realize what is wrong in our lives. It
corrects us when we are wrong and teaches us to do what
is right. God uses it to prepare and equip his people to do
every good work. — 2 Timothy 3:15-17 NLT*

The only question remaining is whether you will trust the coach, or just continue to trust your own swing. I can tell you that God corrects my swing every single day. God is teaching me that what feels good is not always right for me. Applying the new teaching may feel awkward at first—just as learning to swing right may not feel natural—but eventually it will become second nature. I've learned that if I trust in what God says, the mechanics and follow-through will become natural—and God will begin to work in amazing ways. If I just go with what I feel, I typically miss, but if I go with what He is telling me, I typically hit the mark and do greater things in my life. That life is built upon trust. Listen up! Be coached to greatness.

Fight with Scripture. Hope is here because Jesus has come. We can confidently approach God, clothed in righteousness. Will you make a choice to enter His presence and learn from the Master? The Word of God is not an antique to be left gathering dust on a shelf somewhere. It is not to be misunderstood or misused. It's a Word that is applicable to your life every moment, every day, and in every area—if you will learn to use it properly.

The Word of God is referred to as a sword (Ephesians 6:17; Hebrews 4:12). Many Christians worry about what they said, what they heard, or what they felt. The Bible tells us to take every thought captive to Christ (2 Corinthians 10:5). We can use the Word of God to defend ourselves and to fight off negativity in our lives.

If you're experiencing negativity or a condemning force in your life, it is not from God. God is not negative; He uses positive reinforcement, and He is a positive influence. When negativity comes toward you, get out your sword and fight it off. Fight using the Scripture! The enemy has no place in your life if you are a believer in Jesus Christ. If you listen to the voice of the opponent, he will get in your head. And if the opponent gets in your head, he will get into your heart. And if he gets into your heart, he will begin to manifest in your actions. And if he gets into your actions, you will be defeated, discouraged, and depressed. Hope will be drained from your life.

Instead, listen to the voice of the Almighty God. Renew your mind with His Word! Read it and understand that He is for you, not against you. The creator of the universe only has your best intentions at heart. His love never fails. Negativity has no place in your life. You cut it out. You put it out. Remember, God is for you, not against you. Trust Him. Let hope arise!

The enemy is opposed to the God in you. He doesn't care about you. He wants to stop your communication with God. He doesn't want you to understand who God truly is. He doesn't want you to be equipped with the truth found in God's Word; the enemy wants you to miss the mark. He doesn't want you to fulfill your destiny. He wants to try to tell you who you are, instead of you believing what God says about you.

The Bible assures us, "He who is in you is greater than he who is in the world" (1 John 4:4 NKJV). When you begin to claim that truth and live out of who He is in you, you fight the world off with your sword, the Word of God. Listen up. Obey the Word of God. You will be inspired and coach others to greatness.

If you will begin to be responsible for yourself and to influence others, God will begin to open doors to success in your life that you never dreamed about, thought about, or imagined (Ephesians 3:20). God is an amazing God. He wants you to sink the shot. He wants you to get in the Word and listen up.

Take Action

The last thing you have to do is swing! *Take action* with what you have heard from God's Word. James urges us:

> But don't just listen to God's word. You must do what it says. Otherwise, you are only fooling yourselves. For if you listen to the word and don't obey, it is like glancing at your face in a mirror. You see yourself, walk away, and forget what you look like. But if you look carefully into the perfect law that sets you free, and if you do what it says and don't forget what you heard, then God will bless you for doing it.
> — *James 1:22-25 NLT*

Listening without acting is useless!

The circle of commitment. God doesn't want you to just hit the ball, He wants you to sink the shot. The difference between a professional golfer and an amateur is that amateurs typically hit around 95 or 100 on the golf course. If you're like me, you hit 128. Professionals are hitting in the 60s. The secret is this: they believe in what they know and they put it into practice.

On the golf course it's called the *circle of commitment*. The professional golfer knows which club to pull out for each particular circumstance. They've experienced it, they have knowledge of it, and they know what the club is supposed to do. The moment they pull it out of the bag, they are committed to using that club because they've already listened up, they've already analyzed the shot and understood how far it is to the hole. Once they pull that club out, they are committed to taking action with it.

Some of us waver. We don't know which club to use. We might even walk back to the bag to switch clubs. We lack commitment. We just like the game and want to hit the ball. But we need to have a deeper purpose behind our swing.

Call the shot. Another difference between a professional and an amateur is that they don't want to just hit the ball—*they actually call the shot.* They speak it into existence. They declare it because they know what is true. They will pull the club out and say, "I'm getting ready to hit that ball with this club, toward that hole, in order to sink the shot. I'm going to hit it with a 15-degree turn on it. I'm going to hit it 20 feet off the ground, and it's going to land 140 feet down the course."

They call that shot before they even pull the club out of the bag. They've listened up and they believe it. They take action with what they know. They declare it, trust it, and go for it. They don't have 100 percent control over the outcome, but they believe the outcome based on knowledge and experience.

God wants us all to call the shot, not just randomly hit the ball and hope it goes somewhere. Shots can be called in every area of our lives. God doesn't just want to forgive you of the misses, He wants you to hit the mark of His incredible standard for your life. Our job is to listen up, and then by faith take action. Swing the club and believe that God will do what He says He will do!

The gap of faith. Hope is here because Jesus has come. For those who have believed, God resides with us and in us. He coaches us daily through His Holy Spirit. The Holy Spirit works on our behalf as we begin to get instruction from God's Word. The Spirit of God works in us; all we have to do is commit by faith and call the shot. Some of us need to declare what is true. Declare it in your marriage today! Declare God's truth when you wake up tomorrow morning! Declare what is true in your financial situation!

You may comprehend the truth with your mind, but still get hung up. There is a gap you may be overlooking called the *gap of faith.* Faith is believing and having full confidence and hope in what you cannot yet see (Hebrews 11:1). It's trusting that God will do what He says He will do. God is not asking us to participate in all this activity so we can prove something to Him. God is asking us to participate so that we learn to embrace Him and trust Him. Then we will begin to understand that God does what He says He will do!

He is an amazing God. He is a God who is for you, not against you. He says that we have all missed the mark, but He came to do something to make up the distance. I encourage you to loosen up. I encourage you to listen up. I encourage you to take action with faith and swing your club! God leaves us with some promises in Proverbs:

> *Trust in the Lord with all your heart; do not depend on your own understanding. Seek his will in all you do, and he will show you which path to take. Don't be impressed with your own wisdom. Instead, fear the Lord and turn away from evil. Then you will have healing for your body and strength for your bones. Honor the Lord with your wealth and with the best part of everything you produce. Then he will fill your barns with grain, and your vats will overflow with good wine.* —**Proverbs 3:5-10 NLT**

Some of us are confused, at a crossroads. We don't know which path to take. The Bible tells us to trust in God, not ourselves. Begin to seek who He says He is, and who He says you are, and He will show you which path to take. When we trust and follow God, our lives will be prosperous and filled with joy. Trust the good coach. Trust that He has accepted you, that you're highly valued, and that His Word will equip you to walk with Him. You will sink the shot because hope is here!

Get Cheerleaders

Though trust and obedience toward God are sufficient for us, He intends for us to find people who will motivate us, encourage us, and challenge us to rise up. That's what the Church is. It's not a place of condemnation—there is "no condemnation for those who are in Christ Jesus" (Romans 8:1 ESV). It's a place of inspiration, encouragement, and motivation. The Church is supposed to challenge you to rise up.

So what is a real cheerleader? Someone who *encourages* you, not *enables* you. Don't surround yourself with people who influence you to focus on the problem. Many self-help groups fall into this trap by enabling each other to focus on their problems above the God who should be the central focus. You need people who see more in you than you see in yourself, who want you to rise up and become all that God has created you to be. These cheerleaders don't sit around and continually focus on the problem; they give you the solution to the problem, encourage you to embrace that solution, and help you live out life to its fullest potential. It is a shame that so many people are caught up in enablement—to the detriment of the Church.

The Scriptures tell us, "And let us not neglect our meeting together, as some people do, but encourage one another, especially now that the day of his return is drawing near" (Hebrews 10:25 NLT).

Study groups are a great place to find cheerleaders who encourage you, motivate you, and inspire the God-potential in you. They will do life with you constantly, consistently, all the time—through ups and downs. They will talk about the solution to the problem, the mission of our Great God, and the fulfillment of God's plan in our cities and in our culture. Life Groups will provide you with a place to study God's Word with other believers who want to cooperate with God and reach their full potential. They revitalize the body of Christ for the work God has set before them. God never called you to stay small; God called you to rise up and become the great person that He has created you to be.

Participate!

Ultimately, then, living out your hope requires your participation. Participation erupts our hope. When you participate, you allow God to use you to change the world. As He uses you, the hope inside of you will rise up.

We participate by using the unique gifts God has given us. The Bible calls them "spiritual gifts" (1 Peter 4:10). God gives us these deposits to motivate and encourage people. When I see people changed through the use of my gifts, I know it is because of God. On my own, I would screw something up. I'm a mess. But God can work through me, and He can work through you. We seek to instill hope so that the gifts God has deposited in you will begin to rise.

You may not feel like you are qualified, but God working through you will change the world. Let Him come alive. Unleash the hope in your life. When we use our gifts to partner with God, lives are changed. It is amazing how God uses us to build His Kingdom.

God has given you a gift to encourage others. As you participate and encourage others, you will be encouraged. Courage will be infused within you. Believe that God will do what He says He will do. Participate, and watch the hope start to erupt in your life!

WORKBOOK

Chapter 2 Questions

Question: Where do you fall short spiritually? To what extent are you letting God help? To what extent are you relying on yourself?

_____

_____

_____

_____

_____

_____

_____

_____

_____

_____

_____

Question: In what ways do you need to loosen up, spiritually speaking? What structures do you need to let go of? How can you refocus on Jesus?

_____

_____

_____

_____

_____

_____

_____

_____

_____

_____

_____

_____

Question: In what ways do you need to listen up to God and His Word? In what situations are you using the right tools? In which areas of your life do you need to listen more carefully to God and perhaps use different tools?

_____

_____

_____

_____

_____

_____

_____

_____

_____

_____

_____

_____

Question: Are you taking action? What further or different action do you need to take to live out your hope and faith in God? How can you commit more fully to Him in your daily life and lean more fully on the Holy Spirit?

_____

_____

_____

_____

_____

_____

_____

_____

_____

_____

Question: Who are your cheerleaders—and who should be your cheerleaders? How can you cultivate deeper ties with the right cheerleaders?

_____

_____

_____

_____

_____

_____

_____

_____

_____

_____

_____

Action: Recognize that you don't measure up on your own merits, but let God be your coach and take up the slack. Loosen up; rest in Jesus instead of focusing on the law, the structures of religion, and the mechanics of faith. Listen up, relying on Scripture and believing fully that God's way is best so you can be sure to use the right tool for each situation. Then take action in confidence, committing your ways to the Lord and leaning on the Holy Spirit for wisdom. Finally, find the right cheerleaders, especially in the Church. In all things, even as you stand on God's grace, be an active participant in living out your faith and hope.

Chapter 2 Notes

_____

_____

_____

_____

_____

_____

_____

_____

_____

_____

_____

_____

_____

_____

_____

_____

_____

_____

_____

_____

_____

_____

CHAPTER THREE

Unlocking the Kingdom

Knowing your true identity will change your life. When you begin to understand the God whom you belong to, everything about you will be affected. Your attitude, actions, demeanor, and countenance will change. The innate knowledge that you are loved, valued, and precious will overflow within. You will accomplish amazing things with your life. And you will bring the very presence of the King everywhere you go.

Humble your heart and come before the creator to claim your true identity! Strengthen your stance, push the enemy back, and exhibit God in the world! Put on the full armor of God by recognizing who you are in Christ. He is your salvation. He is your righteousness. He is the truth. He has made peace between you and God.

God's truth is simple, but the enemy tries to complicate it. He wants to define you. He doesn't want you to grasp the truth, because the truth is detrimental to his influence. It strips him of power. Silence the enemy by trusting fully in God's simple truth. Become like a child, and put all your faith and trust into His promises and provision. If you want to be great in the Kingdom of Heaven, humble yourself to become like a child again.

Jesus tells us to become like children, but later Paul encourages us to be mature. He says, "When I was a child, I spoke and thought and reasoned as a child. But when I grew up, I put away childish things" (1 Corinthians 13:11 NLT). So which is it? How can both be true?

The answer is that we need to be child*like*, while putting childish ways behind us. We need to approach God with the humble heart of a trusting child, but we also need to learn from Him, grow, mature, and leave foolishness behind. There are some things we go through that we might not yet understand. We have limited vision, like a child ignorant of the ways of the world. God is our loving Father who knows what's best for us, and He calls us to trust Him with the bigger picture. He calls us to trust like children—but mature children who are able to see by faith. When we see and live by faith, we have to learn how to use the keys God gives, even as we let go of other things that distract us from Him.

Hidden Keys

Imagine that you had a million dollars locked in a safe hidden in your bedroom. Would you tell a stranger where you put the key to that safe? Unless you were crazy, you wouldn't—because the stranger could just knock you on the head, take your key, and steal your money! The place where you hide your keys should be heavily guarded and safe from threat—because without the key, you have no access to the money. It becomes worthless.

If you've ever lost a set of important keys, you understand their value. You can't drive your car without your car keys. You can't enter your house without your house keys. Without the keys to access something, you are not able to fully appreciate its value.

Likewise, God has great things in store for each of us. Our true destinies are hidden with Christ in God (Colossians 3:3). God has also given us the keys to access these things. We can unlock our futures and live as who we were created to be!

It is available to every single one of us—but many people don't even realize they have access to this incredible set of keys. We have an enemy who wants to hide the keys. He knows that if we discover the keys, he is powerless over us. He wants to maintain control. He wants to mask the immensely valuable gift available to us—so that it becomes worthless. If we don't realize that we have access to the gift, and utilize it, it becomes useless to us.

Jesus came to expose the keys. Jesus came to give us access to abundant life. Jesus invites us to live in the Kingdom, here and now. Matthew records a conversation between Jesus and His disciples:

When Jesus came to the region of Caesarea Philippi, he asked his disciples, "Who do people say that the Son of Man is?"

"Well," they replied, "some say John the Baptist, some say Elijah, and others say Jeremiah or one of the other prophets."

Then he asked them, "But who do you say I am?"

Simon Peter answered, "You are the Messiah, the Son of the living God." — Matthew 16:13-16 NLT

The moment Peter answered the question correctly, Jesus began to help him understand his own identity. It's one thing to know who Jesus is, but it takes things to a whole new level once you let Jesus tell you who you are. After Peter identified Jesus as the Messiah, Jesus replied:

You are blessed, Simon son of John, because my Father in heaven has revealed this to you. You did not learn this from any human being. Now I say to you that you are Peter (which means "rock"), and upon this rock I will build my church, and all the powers of hell will not conquer it. And I will give you the keys of the Kingdom of Heaven. Whatever you forbid on earth will be forbidden in heaven, and whatever you permit on earth will be permitted in heaven." — Matthew 16:17-19 NLT

Jesus told Peter that He would build a great people based on Peter's answer and based on who Jesus described Peter to be. Darkness will not hold this kind of Church back. As we understand our identities in Christ, we are given access to the Kingdom of Heaven!

Peter had been a disciple of Jesus for over two years, and had *just* identified who Jesus was. He was only beginning to understand his own identity in Christ. Sometimes it takes a little time for us to understand who

we are. Many people today remain in that phase of life—
they know who Jesus is but haven't yet uncovered their
own destiny, their own purpose in life. They don't yet
fully understand God's plan for them.

There are a set of keys for you today, just as there
were for Peter. Jesus has given us keys to the Kingdom!
He has given us the means to grasp our destinies, here
and now. We only have to understand the keys to take a
hold of this truth.

Greatness in the Kingdom of Heaven

A few chapters after Jesus tells Peter about the keys to
the Kingdom, the disciples ask about the Kingdom of
Heaven. Jesus exposes to them what Kingdom life is all
about:

> *About that time the disciples came to Jesus and asked,
> "Who is greatest in the Kingdom of Heaven?"*
>
> *Jesus called a little child to him and put the child among
> them. Then he said, "I tell you the truth, unless you turn
> from your sins and become like little children, you will
> never get into the Kingdom of Heaven. So anyone who
> becomes as humble as this little child is the greatest in the
> Kingdom of Heaven. — Matthew 18:1-4 NLT*

Many times we are critical of the question the
disciples asked—but their desire to go to God to ask how
to be great was a good desire. They didn't quite
understand the Kingdom and they didn't yet comprehend
what God had in store for them, so they asked Jesus

about it. However, the answer Jesus gave must have come as a surprise: He told them to become like children in order be great in the Kingdom of Heaven.

Have you ever noticed how innately trusting children are? We have to teach them about "stranger danger" because a kid is likely to run up to the meanest looking person, wanting to be friends. They'll talk to anyone off the street regardless of what they look like or smell like—oblivious of potential harm. So in order to keep our kids safe, we teach them not to trust anybody! It becomes programmed into our minds because of the type of world we live in. If we don't keep our guards up, we could get hurt.

Against our better judgment, Jesus tells us to become like little children. He asks us to trust Him with the pure, unquestioning trust of a child. A little child trusts wholly. A little child loves fully. A little child is always learning. Children know something about experiencing life abundantly!

After Jesus revealed to the disciples how the Kingdom worked, they needed to be reminded again. Matthew records a subsequent conversation between Jesus and His disciples:

> One day some parents brought their children to Jesus so he could lay his hands on them and pray for them. But the disciples scolded the parents for bothering him.
>
> But Jesus said, "Let the children come to me. Don't stop them! For the Kingdom of Heaven belongs to those who are like these children." And he placed his hands on their heads and blessed them before he left. — **Matthew 19:13-15 NLT**

Jesus told them again that the Kingdom of Heaven belongs to little children. He wants us to become like children and welcome those around us. The keys have a purpose. We are called to bring others to Christ! Jesus rebuked His disciples for keeping the children from coming.

You don't have to be on the defense. You don't have to have it all figured out. Put your guard down. Love, live, and learn without holding back. Hope is here. We can receive the keys to the Kingdom of Heaven when we become like children again.

Jesus tells us again in Matthew: "So if you sinful people know how to give good gifts to your children, how much more will your heavenly Father give good gifts to those who ask him" (Matthew 7:11 NLT). The things He has in store for us will not disappoint. If we place all of our trust in Him, we will not end up regretting it.

Don't Mishandle the Keys

Jesus teaches us what the keys are all about. He also warns us of what the keys are *not* about. Luke records His warning to the Pharisees and religious leaders of the day:

> *What sorrow awaits you experts in religious law! For you remove the key to knowledge from the people. You don't enter the Kingdom yourselves, and you prevent others from entering.* — *Luke 11:52 NLT*

The religious teachers chose not to enter the Kingdom. They did not have the trusting hearts of little children. They thought they had already learned it all. Worst of all, they prevented others from accessing the very key they were abusing. They led others away from the Kingdom of Heaven! This is not how to handle the keys. Jesus came to open the way to the Kingdom, and the religious leaders were barring others from entering.

Jesus has no patience for those abusing the keys. He called out the Pharisees in public, showing His disciples and those who were listening that their religious leaders were misusing the keys. They were leading others astray, and would be held accountable for it. The keys Jesus gave His disciples would impact families and communities in the unseen future. They held the potential to change the world! Jesus came to expose the keys! He shows us how to unlock our destinies in God. He gave us the "key to knowledge" that has been passed down through the ages, from generation to generation. He wants us to accomplish the amazing things He has planned for our lives!

Don't let the enemy blind you to the reality of the Kingdom. He doesn't want you to understand the future that God has in store for you. He wants to keep you out of the King's presence. Become like a child again and gain full access to the Kingdom. Believe in Jesus as the Son of the Living God, that He gave His life on the cross, and that He conquered the grave. Believe the truth about Jesus, and let Him teach you about yourself. Let Him bring you to your own destiny in this world. The enemy tries to hide the keys, but Jesus exposes them to the world! He helps us discover the truth of who we are, so that we can bring others into His presence.

Total Access

It would be awful to have access to something as great as what Jesus freely offers us—and not access it to accomplish what God has planned for us! Are you using the keys? Are you accessing what God is offering you? Many of Jesus's teachings centered on the Kingdom. The Kingdom is here on Earth because you and I—sons and daughters of the King—are here. Jesus lives through us! We may not even fully understand what we're unleashing. Consequently we may be missing out on life.

After the resurrection of Jesus, He spent some time on Earth. Luke tells us:

> *During the forty days after he suffered and died, he appeared to the apostles from time to time, and he proved to them in many ways that he was actually alive. And he talked to them about the Kingdom of God.* — *Acts 1:3 NLT*

For forty days in His resurrected body, Jesus taught His disciples what Kingdom life was all about. He spoke of the Kingdom of God because He wanted to instill in them what it meant to have keys to the Kingdom. He wanted to equip them for the amazing things God had planned. They needed to be prepared for the privilege given to them—for the work of drawing others into the Kingdom. Likewise, we need to understand exactly what it means to have keys to the Kingdom.

At its core, having keys to the Kingdom means that we have *total access*—we have total access to the creator of the Universe and His wisdom. Godly wisdom will begin to reveal to you how to live life. It will teach you what's important and what's not important. It will give you purpose. There is no limit to the number of ways godly wisdom can be applied. It will teach you how to parent your children, how to steward everything God has placed in your hands, how to handle your money, and how to approach your relationships.

When you become a Kingdom citizen, the same power that resurrected Jesus from the grave will be available to walk you through life (Romans 8:11). What power are you living by? When you begin to walk in His power and seek after godly wisdom, you become like a little child. You go to God and say, "Daddy, I don't understand it all. I'm frustrated—but I'm trying hard and I'm willing to learn!" Your heavenly Father won't leave you disappointed. He will speak to you and fashion a renewed sense of purpose in you. He'll give you a big, honking key and tell you that you've got full access. Never get too smart to access the wisdom of your heavenly Father.

The curtain was torn; we have full access to God! We can gain heavenly wisdom. Why would you settle for anything less when the King's perfect provision is available? Don't try to provide for yourself. Don't rely on other people for fulfillment. We can go to our heavenly Father to figure out how to do every single area of life. If you will come into His presence like a child, trust in what He says, and learn from Him, you will start living as He says you can live, and loving the way He says you can love.

Stumbling Blocks

From time to time, there may be things that try to hinder our access to what we have through Christ. It is helpful to understand them so that we can properly combat them when they come our way.

Being Under Satan's Yolk

Many people are confused and held back by situations they've created. Do you know anyone who is held back by busyness? They mistake their own need to fill their lives up with activity for God. Being too busy is actually a deviation from God's will, and can work in favor of the enemy. Being "busy" can be synonymous with Being Under Satan's Yolk. We need to stay *focused*, not busy. We are to focus on what God wants us to do in the world, not fill our lives up with meaningless activity. Even if the things we replace God with are "good" or "godly" things, they will not satisfy us if they are not what God has intended for us. Joy will be drained from our lives. When we stay focused on what God has for us, we keep childlike joy and wonder in our lives.

Sometimes we try to serve God in order to repay Him for what He has done for us. We stay *busy,* serving God like slaves. But God is not looking for servants; He is searching for sons and daughters. The Bible tells us that the angels in heaven serve God. Powers and principalities fall under His sovereignty. Even the devil serves God's purpose in this world.

Without proper understanding on our part, we will misinterpret Scripture. Paul tells us to be slaves to Christ (1 Corinthians 7:22), and he identifies himself as a slave to Christ (Romans 1:1). But the type of slave Paul was talking about is called a *bond slave*. A bond slave was comparable to the son or daughter of a King. Bond slaves believed so much in the master that they would willingly become part of his household. They would have complete trust in the master's ability to take care of them. It was a loving relationship, not a forced situation.

When the Bible speaks of being slaves to Christ, it is talking about a place of great freedom. Being a slave to Christ means loving Him so much that serving Him is an utter joy. It is the place where we find our greatest fulfillment. It is a place reserved for God's own children.

Don't overcomplicate it. Don't give up the freedom found in serving God as a son or daughter for the busyness of filling your life with meaningless diversions. Jesus came to give us abundant life. He gives us hope. He wants to give us a set of keys allowing us to walk in freedom. Simply believe and accept this.

The enemy comes up with strategies to distort people's understanding of God. He wants us to serve God as hopeless slaves, not as joyful sons and daughters. In Jesus's day, there were two prevalent cultural barriers holding people back. Some were misled by gender. In the Middle Eastern culture at the time, women had no worth or value. Jesus came and boldly challenged this belief. He taught that gender doesn't bar you from becoming a child of God. He called both male and female to Him. Paul tells us, "There is no longer Jew or Gentile, slave or free, male and female. For you are all one in Christ Jesus" (Galatians 3:28 NLT).

Many people also believed that only the Israelites were called to be children of God. Gentiles might have falsely believed that God had no compassion for them. There are numerous times during the ministry of Jesus where He corrected this deceptive mindset. One striking example is when Jesus preached in the synagogue at Nazareth, His hometown. At one point Jesus spoke of God's favor for those outside Israel:

> *Certainly there were many needy widows in Israel in Elijah's time, when the heavens were closed for three and a half years, and a severe famine devastated the land. Yet Elijah was not sent to any of them. He was sent instead to a foreigner—a widow of Zarephath in the land of Sidon. And many in Israel had leprosy in the time of the prophet Elisha, but the only one healed was Naaman, a Syrian.* — **Luke 4:25-27 NLT**

The Jews were so angry when they heard Jesus that they sought to throw Him off a cliff! Jesus wasn't afraid to go against deeply held cultural norms. He corrected the people's twisted understandings. He revealed our identities as children of God, not slaves.

The Enforcer

If you have believed in Jesus as the resurrected Messiah, you have a set of keys. There is nothing that you can do to keep yourself from coming in. There's nothing you can do to thwart that access. Your Father will always welcome you into His presence. You cannot screw up enough to bar your own access, because the authority of the One who gave you the keys is greater than your works. He wants you to enter in and receive the great things in store for you.

Did you ever have to use a hall pass in grade school? It's something you never wanted to be caught without! I had this teacher in elementary school whom we called "the enforcer." Ms. McElroy loved to enforce the rules and catch kids out in the halls who didn't have permission to be there. I would look forward to those few occasions when the principal had given me my hall pass. Ms. McElroy would always come up and try to reprimand me, but I'd say, "*No*, Ms. McElroy, you don't understand." She would inevitably counter back, "Yes, I do understand. You know the rules, son." Then I'd explain that the principal had given me my hall pass to go from here to there—and nothing could stand in the way of his authority!

The enemy is like Ms. McElroy (only symbolically, not personally!). He is the enforcer. He tells you when you've screwed up in life and tries to hold it against you. He'll say, "You've been married four times. You can't come to church. God can't use you." Or, "Don't you remember that kid you bullied when you were fifteen? You can't take those things back. It will taint you for life."

But the King tells a different story. The King says that if you believe in Him, you have total access! You can walk with Him and gain wisdom. He will tell you how to move forward in life. Maybe you need to pull out your "hall pass" occasionally. When something tries to bar your way, remember the authority of the One who gave you the keys. If someone tries to tell you that imperfect people aren't allowed in, let Scripture be your guide—let the words of Jesus be your authority. He says He came to give access to imperfect people—not to those who already have it together (Mark 2:17).

Fine Print

We have been taught that if something is too good to be true, it probably is. In our society today, we encounter so much fine print that we've turned into skeptics. It's everywhere nowadays. You might click something on the Internet offering a "free monthly trial," not knowing that you will be billed for a year unless you manually cancel at the end of that month. You might see a car commercial and go to buy that car, only to find out that in reality the deal isn't as good as it looked on TV. Your spouse might surprise you with a gift and start treating you really nicely, only to find out a week later that it was because they wanted something from you. We constantly look for a catch, because many times there is one.

But this is not so with Jesus! Don't hold back. Don't let your past experiences of hurt and missing the fine print redefine what Jesus has promised you. He says that you've got full access because of His finished work on the cross. He says He's forgiven you of all your misses in life. There is no catch! Too many people stay away from church because they're afraid the church only wants something out of them. Too many people don't take Jesus at His word because they think He can't possibly mean what He says.

We don't have to jump through hoops with Jesus. He says to just trust Him like a child, and enter into His presence. There is no fine print.

Don't be a skeptic. Move forward and step into the presence of your heavenly Father. Learn from Him, and accomplish the greatness that He has in store for you. You're never too old to start learning again. Use your keys to gain access, and invite others to enter in, too!

Understanding Your Stewardship

In life, we experience shortage. And again, we have a hard time not letting our experiences define the way we approach our Father. If we let our worldly mentality run over into our spiritual lives, we become afraid that the King doesn't have enough resources to go around. We doubt His provision, so we try to hoard it whenever it comes, not believing it will be enough. We must realize that with God, there is never any lack. We will not be disappointed when we sacrifice for the sake of Christ. God's blessings are meant to overflow and reach those around us. They are to be shared; we cannot possibly keep this Good News, this full access, these keys to ourselves. We have to understand our stewardship in order to receive God's fullness.

The Bible tells us that *whoever* believes in Jesus will have eternal life and become a son or daughter of God.

John 3:16 says, "For this is how God loved the world: He gave his one and only Son, so that everyone who believes in him will not perish but have eternal life." And the Bible also says that *we* are the means to making this happen. We hold the keys. Paul tells us in Romans:

> For "Everyone who calls on the name of the Lord will be saved." But how can they call on him to save them unless they believe in him? And how can they believe in him if they have never heard about him? And how can they hear about him unless someone tells them? And how will anyone go and tell them without being sent? That is why the Scriptures say, "How beautiful are the feet of messengers who bring good news!" — **Romans 10:13-15 NLT**

Great responsibility comes with our keys. God gives us full access to His presence, but He asks us to usher others into His house. Our job isn't to decide who gets to come in and who doesn't; it is to open the doors wide for anyone who happens to walk by! Jesus wants us to welcome others on His behalf. Like little kids, He wants us to invite people over. Ushering people into the Kingdom means treating them with great value, meeting them where they are, and getting them in a seat so the King can equip them for life.

You are a steward. You have total access to the King—but it's beyond you. It's beyond me. When we step up and serve in the local church, we are showing evidence of what God has done in our lives. Someone will come to you for counsel. Someone will come to you for wisdom. Someone will come to you to see the King.

You are a key holder, so open the doors and give them full access!

Unlock Prosperity

Jesus told the Parable of the Lost Son to demonstrate the love and compassionate heart of our Father. Luke 15 records the story: There was a very rich father who had two sons. One of his sons came to him and asked to have his inheritance early. The father obliged and gave his son the inheritance. The son took the wealth and left home, seeking to unlock his own destiny and make his own way through life. Eventually, he found himself alone, broke, and out of options. The Bible says he decided to return home and apologize to his father. He braced himself for rebuke, but instead was greeted by a father who had his eye on the horizon, looking for him, hoping for his return. The father saw his son from a long way off and ran to embrace him. He walked with him into the house and told all the servants that his son had returned home, and to prepare a celebration feast. The father clothed his son with sandals, a ring, and a robe, and celebrated his return with the whole household.

Our heavenly Father treats us like this. He welcomes us when we have done nothing but squander the gifts He has given us. He longs for us to return home and understand how loved we are. He has His eye on the horizon, always looking for the day when we will humble our hearts and return to His loving embrace. He celebrates the recovery of every lost sheep. He gives us keys to His Kingdom.

Jesus also talks about the other son in the parable, the one who had remained home the whole time. He was jealous because of the grand welcome his brother had received after wasting his entire inheritance. The father tells this son that he has full access to everything he owns. He is happy his son never left home, but is also happy to celebrate the return of his lost son.

The second son represents the highly religious people who keep all the rules but miss out on what God is really about. God wants children, not performers. He wants kids who will trust Him, learn from Him, and love Him. The second son had been working the whole time under his father as a slave, not as a child.

No matter where you've been or what you've done, God is not going to close the doors on you. That's not who He is. Instead, because He saw that we were enslaved to sin and living in darkness, He put on flesh and came to Earth as a man, to show how much He loved and cared for us—even while we were sinners. He gave His own life on the cross and defeated the power of sin, once and for all. He rose from the grave to show His own power and control in the face of an enemy who tries to blind us to reality. And He looks at you and asks you to become as a child and trust Him. God wants you to come home to Him.

You are totally accepted. You are highly valued, and you have been equipped to do greater things. Hope has come—His name is Jesus, and He has given you a set of keys. Therefore, enter in and access your King. Unlock your destiny. Usher others into the presence of the King, and He will speak to them. Unlock prosperity in your community by exposing people to the King of kings and the Lord of lords. Open the doors to receive wisdom from on high! Jesus is raising up a Church that will expel darkness and reveal light—and the gates of hell cannot hold it back. Hope is here!

WORKBOOK

Chapter 3 Questions

Question: What are the keys to God's Kingdom that Jesus offers us?

_____

_____

_____

_____

_____

_____

_____

_____

_____

_____

_____

Question: How successful are you at maintaining childlike humility? In what relationships or areas of your life do you need to work on cultivating such humility—and how will you do so?

_____

_____

_____

_____

_____

_____

_____

_____

_____

_____

_____

_____

_____

Question: Are you making the most of the keys Jesus has given you? In what ways could you make more of your access to the Kingdom?

_____

_____

_____

_____

_____

_____

_____

_____

_____

_____

_____

_____

Question: What spiritual stumbling blocks are particularly challenging to you? Where has busyness crept into your life, and how can you refocus on God and His grace?

_____

_____

_____

_____

_____

_____

_____

_____

_____

_____

_____

_____

Question: What great things might God be calling you to do?

_____

_____

_____

_____

_____

_____

_____

_____

_____

_____

_____

_____

Action: Embrace your identity as God's child by cultivating childlike humility toward Him. Don't mishandle the keys to God's Kingdom by making others believe they have to earn those keys, and don't rest your identity on religious prescription. Check your urge to earn the grace that God gives you freely. Recognize the stumbling blocks in your life, making sure the enemy isn't keeping you busy instead of focused on God and His plans for you.

Chapter 3 Notes

_____

_____

_____

_____

_____

_____

_____

_____

_____

_____

_____

_____

_____

_____

_____

_____

_____

_____

_____

_____

_____

_____

_____

CHAPTER FOUR

Taking Ground

In Egypt, all who applied the blood of the lamb to their doorposts were spared. Death bypassed their households. They lived to see another day and were led toward a life of abundance found in the Promised Land. They were initially excited to be moving from oppression to the promise, but they overlooked the journey they would need to take through the wilderness (Exodus 14:11). God still required their faith, trust, and hope. He had a plan to provide for their daily needs. He knew exactly how to bring them to where they needed to be. Through the challenges they faced in the wilderness, God was preparing them to receive the promise.

Likewise, the purpose of your journey is to prepare you to receive the promise. Don't give up in the wilderness because you think everything should come easily and without needing to trust in God. Understand that there are challenges placed in your life to build you up, strengthen your faith, and equip you to receive all that God has to offer. God has a plan to move you from a place of bondage to an abundant, eternal life, but there is a wilderness in between. You have to trust in God's plan, and place all your hope in Jesus. The resulting life of faith will carry you to the promise.

The Israelites were moving from oppression to this incredible place of promise, but even after they reached the Promised Land, there were still battles to win. The land had to be cleared of Israel's enemies. Israel needed to drive out evil and claim their inheritance. Crossing into the Promised Land didn't permanently end all their struggles, but as long as they trusted in God, the Israelites would succeed in taking ground. With all their trust placed in God, He would guarantee their success (Joshua 1:6-9).

There are battles for you to face as well. Living a life of abundance found in God doesn't mean that struggles are nonexistent. We may still face financial difficulties, sickness, temptation, and countless other forms of oppression, but when we place our hope in God, He provides. Hope is here. Hope has made a provision for us. Hope has a plan for our lives, even in the midst of struggle.

If you put all your hope in God's plan for your life, challenges will begin to diminish. Faith will increase and you will move forward and take ground, just as the Israelites advanced farther and farther into the Promised Land. There is a cosmic plan, a spiritual dimension to your life. When you rise above your immediate circumstances and understand God's plan, the blessings of God will be unleashed. Hope will set you free. Hope will activate your faith so that you can take more ground.

Get Dressed for Success

As believers, we have this incredible hope that we can bank our lives on. Learning how to store up that hope so that we are empowered to take action will literally change the lives of those around us. We are called to bring hope to the oppressed and set the captives free!

Don't misunderstand what the Christian life is. Surrendering to Jesus doesn't mean you won't face challenges or struggles. In fact, Jesus tells us that in this world we will have troubles (John 16:33). We will face different trials. It rains on the just and the unjust alike (Matthew 5:45). But when we surrender to Jesus, God equips us to face everything that comes our way. We can stand firm during trials and even take ground for the Kingdom.

We need to put on the full armor of God so that we are equipped for oncoming battles. There is a real spiritual war being waged against us every day. The dark powers of this world are not content to sit idly by while you bring hope to others and spread the Good News—that is why you need to put on your armor *daily.*

Paul tells us, "Therefore, put on every piece of God's armor so you will be able to resist the enemy in the time of evil" (Ephesians 6:13 NLT). The enemy wants to knock us off course and take away our purpose. Our purpose is to bring hope and prosperity to a suffering world, to a world blinded by darkness. Put on your armor, stand firm, and resist the enemy so that you can accomplish your purpose. Don't let him take your purpose from you! Get dressed daily.

Salvation is a gift from God (Ephesians 3:9). It's not a gift you put on the shelf; it's a gift you use every day. It's not a gift that just gets you into heaven; it's a gift that puts you in a right relationship with your heavenly Father so you can move forward in life. It's a gift that we are to use right now by putting on the armor of God.

Get Dressed with Purpose

People put on outfits with a purpose all the time. Athletes put on uniforms to accomplish their purpose of winning. They dress themselves to be fully prepared to face the challenges that lay ahead. You would never see a professional football player go on the field without his shoulder pads on. He'd get creamed!

And have you ever seen the outfit of a NASCAR driver? They dress to prepare themselves for battle. When you have drivers going 200 miles per hour, bumper to bumper, for three hours straight, anything could happen. NASCAR drivers wear helmets with breathing tubes in them. Their suits can withstand the fire that might break out in a wreck. They ride equipped with these outfits because their car could wind up flipped over against a wall. They get dressed to fulfill their purpose of surviving the battle and winning the race.

Moms and dads also wear a sort of uniform. If you're the parent of a young child, you know what I'm talking about. You don't leave the house ill-prepared to face the day. You go equipped with diapers, bottles, pacifiers, snacks, and an extra change of clothes. Unless you want to have a miserable day, you don't forget to equip yourself with the essentials.

When you wear a fancy outfit or expensive uniform, you have confidence. You look good. You feel good. You believe in yourself because your appearance gives you a sense of worth. How much more should we then trust in the armor that God has given us? By putting on the salvation of God, we acknowledge our value and worth in the eyes of God. We have confidence and hope because we realize Jesus is our righteousness. We stop fighting *for* our lives, and instead fight *from* our lives. Instead of trying to get better, we live in the knowledge that we're already right with God. We already live in His promises. We have the hope, courage, and vision to change our communities, our workplaces, our schools. We begin to influence the world and fulfill our purpose.

If you've ever paid a high price for a fancy outfit, you're going to wear it with pride. You're not going to forget about it in the back of the closet, but instead will sport it everywhere you go. We, as believers, have a uniform to put on. And it's an expensive outfit! Jesus paid a high price so that we could wear it. The Bible says that God has given us His armor. To wear the armor, simply remember every day who you are in Christ, and march toward your purpose wherever you go. Put on your outfit and remember who you are in Christ every single day. Live from that knowledge, and you will begin to accomplish God's purpose for your life.

Get Dressed Daily

Have you ever met someone who keeps their pajamas on all day? Not just for one day, but all the time? Are they usually cheerful and outgoing? No—they don't get up expecting anything special or out of the ordinary to happen. They feel depressed and withdrawn. They don't get dressed, because they don't believe anything great will come their way. There's nothing to prepare for.

Maybe you understand God's provision, but you need some practicality in how to face the challenges put before you. God tells us to dress for success. He gives us a suit of armor so we are prepared to face anything that comes our way. In other words, if you will take off your pajamas and put on your success suit, things will begin to change. You've got to make the decision to get dressed daily. So, what is the suit He is talking about?

Paul preached to the Gentiles in Ephesus:

With the Lord's authority I say this: Live no longer as the Gentiles do, for they are hopelessly confused. Their minds are full of darkness; they wander far from the life God gives because they have closed their minds and hardened their hearts against him. They have no sense of shame. They live for lustful pleasure and eagerly practice every kind of impurity.

*But that isn't what you learned about Christ. Since you have heard about Jesus and have learned the truth that comes from him, **throw off your old sinful nature** and your former way of life, which is corrupted by lust and deception. Instead, let the Spirit renew your thoughts and attitudes. **Put on your new nature**, created to be like God—truly righteous and holy. — **Ephesians 4:17-24 NLT (emphasis added)***

Paul is talking to Gentile Christians, telling them to stop living as Gentiles! He is calling on them to live out their true identities. If he was preaching today, he might say to you, "I know you're surrounded by sinners, by people whose minds are darkened and far from God. It's ingrained into the very culture. But you are no longer a part of that culture. You are a son or daughter of the King. Throw off your old ways and step into the new." Take off your pajamas and put on your success suit, your new nature. Then you will be prepared to take ground.

Your Suit of Armor

Paul also tells us exactly what the suit of armor looks like. He writes these words while imprisoned, and in his physical sight is a Roman soldier. He uses the outfit of the soldier as a metaphor:

A final word: Be strong in the Lord and in his mighty power. Put on all of God's armor so that you will be able to stand firm against all strategies of the devil. For we are not fighting against flesh-and-blood enemies, but against evil rulers and authorities of the unseen world, against mighty powers in this dark world, and against evil spirits in the heavenly places.

*Therefore, put on every piece of God's armor so you will be able to resist the enemy in the time of evil. Then after the battle you will still be standing firm. Stand your ground, putting on the **belt of truth** and the **body armor of God's righteousness**. **For shoes, put on the peace** that comes from the Good News so that you will be fully prepared. In addition to all of these, hold up the **shield of faith** to stop the fiery arrows of the devil. Put on **salvation as your***

> **helmet**, *and take the* **sword of the Spirit**, *which is the word of God.* — **Ephesians 6:10-17 NLT (emphasis added)**

Remember, you are on display to the heavenly realm. Paul tells us that we fight not against flesh and blood, but against rulers, authorities, powers, and evil spirits. That's where the real battle is. We can't rely on earthly tactics, on the wisdom of man, when trying to take ground in the spiritual realm. We must use the equipment that God has given us.

Belt of truth. Every piece of a Roman soldier's armor was fastened to his belt. The belt of truth is the security for every other piece. We are to secure ourselves in the truth. Jesus told us He was the way, the *truth*, and the life (John 14:6). In this day and age, there are many things that *appear* to be true. Our culture tells us that what's true for you is true for you, and what's true for someone else is also true for them; truth is relative to each person. But God tells us that there is only one truth—Christ— and He is a truth in whom we have to ground ourselves.

Body armor of God's righteousness. Some translations say "breastplate of righteousness." Body armor protects your vital organs. The enemy will try to come after your heart, but the body armor—the breastplate—will protect your heart from attack. God's righteousness is not based on what you do; it is only found in Jesus! (Romans 3:22).

Peace for shoes. The shoes of the Roman soldier were sandals with long nails built into them, so that he could get a solid footing to stand against the oncoming enemy. Paul says that peace comes from the Good News. He is saying that the Good News is the foundation for everything, the solid rock we stand upon. God made a provision, and we can have peace in this Good News.

Shield of faith. A shield deflects the fiery arrows of our enemy, the devil. The deception of the enemy is blocked by faith. Our solid hope in Christ activates our faith, allowing us to block the advance of the enemy.

Salvation as a helmet. A helmet covers your head, representing your mind, your way of thinking. Instead of thinking that we have to earn salvation, we realize that it has been given to us. A provision has been made. Wear salvation as a helmet and direct your thoughts to the promises God has given you!

God tells us to dress daily for success. The first five pieces allow us to stand firm, to have a solid defense against the enemy, and the sixth takes us further.

The Final Piece: Take Up Your Sword

Sword of the Spirit. The last piece of God's armor allows us to *take ground*, to move to the offensive. You may be firmly rooted, confident in defending any attack that comes your way, but without the sword of the Spirit you won't receive the full spiritual blessing that God offers you. Without an offensive attack and forward momentum, you won't take any ground. Joshua illustrates what it means to take ground. He held fast to the promises of God. He believed in God's provision and he believed in God's plan, so he took up his sword, advanced into enemy territory, and claimed it for God (see the book of Joshua).

The Word of God allows us to progress. You might have the right equipment to fend off an attack, but you are still in the same stagnant place you were before. There is no growth, no development, and no advancement, because you haven't pulled out your sword to claim the promises of God! You haven't searched the Word to discover what God has promised you, what He says about you, and what He says about the enemy.

Of course, we fend off the arrows of the enemy and hope in a solid foundation for defense, security, and safety; but when you are under oppression, whip out your sword and tell the enemy, "You say I'm a nobody, but God says I'm a child of the King! Get your lies out of my life! I'm taking ground!" Instead of saying, "I'm under attack, I'm trapped, I'm an addict," change your attitude. Speak from the Word: "I'm a son or daughter of the King. I'm no longer an addict. I have overcome by the power of God's Word!"

Understand that you were created for success. Understand that you are a child of the living God, called to fulfill your specific purpose in life. The enemy has no place in your life because hope is here! Apply the Word of God to your life, and watch the enemy flee before you.

There is hope! A provision has been made, a plan is in place. All the equipment you need to succeed has been given to you. Is your hope solid so that your faith can go to work? Shore up your hope in Christ, strengthen your faith, and take some ground!

Children of the Living God

You belong to the Kingdom of God. You are a divine treasure of the all-powerful, all-knowing God. You are the child of the King. A divine treasure is always the devil's target. There is a battle being waged against us. It is unfolding around us every day. Belonging to Christ doesn't mean battles won't come your way; it means the battles will *increase* because the enemy is afraid of what you can do. He wants to stop your purpose and halt your potential. The enemy wants to keep others in darkness and captivity. He doesn't want people to know God and experience His love. He wants to hold our communities hostage. And since we are the means to spreading God's hope, love, and joy, we are targets of the enemy.

The armor of God prepares us. It builds our confidence so that we can reflect Jesus and begin to set captives free in the midst of enemy territory. There are many kinds of captives, but all are in bondage. Some are in bondage to drugs. Some are looking for satisfaction in all the wrong places, hopping from one shaky ground to the next. There are captives in the Church who don't yet comprehend the righteousness they have in Jesus, and are desperately trying to gain God's approval. We are called to set the captives free by being His light in the world.

The Road to Victory

Jesus said, "I am the light of the world. If you follow me, you won't have to walk in darkness, because you will have the light that leads to life" (John 8:12 NLT). We know that Jesus came as a light to others, calling them to Him. He was the light shining in the darkness, and the darkness could not overcome Him (John 1:5). But the Bible also speaks about the light of the world in another place. In the Sermon on the Mount, Jesus told the people:

> *You are the light of the world—like a city on a hilltop that cannot be hidden. No one lights a lamp and then puts it under a basket. Instead, a lamp is placed on a stand, where it gives light to everyone in the house. In the same way, let your good deeds shine out for all to see, so that everyone will praise your heavenly Father.* — **Matthew 5:14-16 NLT**

Paul also tells us: "For once you were full of darkness, but now you have light from the Lord. So live as people of light! For this light within you produces only what is good and right and true" (Ephesians 5:8-9 NLT). And again, Paul reminds us of God's purpose: "I have made you a light to the Gentiles, to bring salvation to the farthest corners of the earth" (Acts 13:47 NLT).

These verses tell us that you and I are the light of the world! The same light that was in Christ shines through those who remain in Him. We are a light to the nations. The light sets the captives free.

God calls us to break the chains of those in bondage, but the enemy is bent on destroying the ones who listen to this calling. The more people who shine with the light of God inside of them, the harder the enemy must work to snuff the light out. He doesn't want the light to spread.

He loves the darkness. When we face the enemy in battle, he probably won't come with a warning sign or trumpet sounds. He uses sneaky tactics. The Bible tells us that he disguises himself as light, so that our own light is deflected (2 Corinthians 11:14). He tries to overpower the light of God in us.

There are three basic schemes the enemy uses to make you lose hope and keep you in darkness: doubting, pouting, and clouting. He tries to make you *doubt* who Jesus is. He encourages you to *pout* about your situation and circumstances. And he tempts you to rely on your own *clout*, thinking you are better than those around you. These are all schemes of the enemy.

Don't avoid one trap only to be ensnared by another! Waywardness and self-righteousness are two sides of the same road, both heading for destruction. Without God, it is a dead-end street. The devil loves to move people from one extreme to the other. There are those in bondage to the flesh, living wild and crazy lives to satisfy their desires. Then once saved, they move to the opposite side of the road and start trying to prove themselves to God. They rely on their own works and become proud. They replace Christ's righteousness with self-righteousness.

Jesus came into the world and divided that road down the middle. He is the straight and narrow way (Matthew 7:14). Don't follow the wayward side of the road, and don't be drawn to the self-righteous side of the road. Don't doubt the work of Jesus, but follow the only One who can lead you to life!

Reflect the Light

Paul describes the narrow road in Corinthians:

Since this new way gives us such confidence, we can be very bold. We are not like Moses, who put a veil over his face so the people of Israel would not see the glory, even though it was destined to fade away. But the people's minds were hardened, and to this day whenever the old covenant is being read, the same veil covers their minds so they cannot understand the truth. And this veil can be removed only by believing in Christ. Yes, even today when they read Moses' writings, their hearts are covered with that veil, and they do not understand.

But whenever someone turns to the Lord, the veil is taken away. For the Lord is the Spirit, and wherever the Spirit of the Lord is, there is freedom. So all of us who have had that veil removed can see and reflect the glory of the Lord. And the Lord—who is the Spirit—makes us more and more like him as we are changed into his glorious image. — 2 **Corinthians 3:12-18 NLT**

The people in Moses's day were not ready for the fullness of God. Moses had to wear a veil because the people could not bear to see the glory of God on his shining face. There was also a veil in place in the Temple separating the Ark of the Covenant in the Holy of Holies from everything else. It prevented a sinful people from entering the presence of a Holy God. Had they entered, the holiness of God would have overwhelmed and even killed them. They weren't yet ready to experience His presence.

But Jesus opened the way for us by tearing the curtain in two! (Matthew 27:51). He calls His Church out of the darkness and into the light. By believing in Jesus, we are able to behold the glory of God. We are free to *see* and *reflect* His glory. Jesus is the Light of the World. Once we are a part of Him, He shines through us and we become lights to the rest of fallen creation! God wants us to see and reflect the light so we can free the captives. People who are held captive in darkness can't see who God is. But when they are drawn to the light, they will begin to understand His nature. When others are drawn to Jesus, they too will be able to see and reflect the light.

The work of the Church is to shine before the rest of the world. God's people are called to reflect His glory while living in the domain of the enemy, so that others would be called out of the darkness. We now have the confidence to fulfill our destinies and help others move forward into theirs.

We are called out so we can see and reflect, but we have to put on our armor every single day. If you forget, the enemy will begin to dull your shine. His strategy is to deceive you and deflect the light in your life. He wants to keep your light from shining. He wants you to forget who you are so that you can't possibly lead others to the truth.

Understand that your armor deflects the arrows so that you can reflect the light. The enemy will search for weak links. If you don't protect yourself with the helmet, breastplate, and shield, you become a weak link for the enemy to manipulate. When you think it's about your good deeds instead of Christ's righteousness, you are a weak link. If you are focused on your own performance, the enemy will keep you busy. You will be his hostage.

By putting on your armor, you free yourself from deception. By remembering who you are in Christ, the enemy will have no foothold!

Whether you are a schoolteacher, stay-at-home mom, or CEO, your job is to be the light wherever you go. The love of God shining through you will set captives free! We have the potential to prosper our communities. We spread the knowledge of Christ so that people recognize who they truly are.

When you put on the armor and fulfill your purpose, your joy will overflow. A peace beyond your own comprehension will settle on your life. Remember who you are in Christ so that you can walk in His fullness every single day!

Send the Enemy Running!

Hope is here not only for me, not only for you, but for the entire world, if only we will put on our armor and live like the light of Jesus every single day.

What holds us back from equipping ourselves to bring others to Christ? What stops us from putting on the full armor of God?

The enemy may use race, age, gender, past mistakes, successful accomplishments—anything he can to hold us back from our God-potential. Jesus, on the contrary, calls us to approach God as children. When Peter recognized who He was, Jesus told Peter that He would raise up a great people (Matthew 16:18). These people would make up the Church. They would understand who Jesus is and who they are, and would live in the world as living testimonies of God. They would use the keys given to them to make a difference, to transform their communities, to reach out to those living in darkness. They would wear their armor daily, equipping themselves to take ground from the enemy and expand the Kingdom of God. They would have joy and hope for all that God has in store for them. This is what we as believers are called to do!

We understand that hope is here to tell us that Jesus forgave all sin on the cross—past, present, and future. Hope tells us that God is completing a work in us, conforming us more and more to His glorious image (2 Corinthians 3:18). But there's even more than that— hope is contagious! It will spread to those around you, shining as a bright beacon and calling others to come. It is proof to the powers and principalities in the universe of God's greatness. We will begin to transform lives for Christ—lives taken from the enemy's own turf!

This should motivate us to face our day-to-day challenges with strength. We will go into our workplaces, our schools, and our neighborhoods focused on Jesus. We will walk away from the things that hinder us and run to pursue our purposes and destinies in life.

As a new creation in Christ Jesus, you are forgiven. Therefore, put on the belt of truth, and understand who you are in Christ. Put on the helmet of salvation, given to you as a gift. Put on your breastplate of righteousness and rest in the finished work of Christ. Put on your shoes, grounding yourself in peace. Block the arrows of the enemy with your shield of faith. And take ground from the enemy, setting captives free with your sword of the Spirit.

Children of Hope

Look at yourself in the mirror and remind yourself of your true identity. You are the light of the world because Jesus is your salvation. He is your righteousness. He is the one who brings you hope and peace. Every day that you get up and put on the armor of God, the devil will be on the run. As soon as your feet touch the floor in the morning, he'll be saying, "Oh crud, they just got up! They just got out their armor and they're putting it on!" It is true that you live in the territory of the enemy, but that's exactly why he's in trouble. Hope is here, and when you live in that hope, you remind the enemy that he does not have a future or a destiny or a hope. Jesus is the way, the truth, and the life (John 14:6). Hope is here!

I want you to win the race of life. Paul says, "I have fought the good fight, I have finished the race, and I have remained faithful" (2 Timothy 4:7). What did he mean? He means he stood against the strategies of the devil. He represented who God called him to be in the world. He understood that this world was not his home, that he was just passing through. He placed all his hope in Jesus, took ground from the enemy, and set the captives free.

When you get dressed daily in the armor of faith and live in the righteousness of Christ, you will live in hope. You will be a light and you will set captives free. Hope will transform all areas of your life! It will touch your marriage, your finances, your coworkers, your classmates—it will follow you wherever you go.

So, knowing that you are a child of God, put on your armor every day and stand firm against the strategies of the enemy. Recognize who you are in Christ and live that hope out in the world. Hope is here. Jesus has come, and He is coming again!

WORKBOOK

Chapter 4 Questions

Question: What are the pieces of spiritual armor with which God equips us? How, specifically, should you dress for success every day? Are there any chinks in your armor—and if so, where?

_____

_____

_____

_____

_____

_____

_____

_____

_____

_____

_____

_____

Question: How can you use the sword of truth—the Word of God—to drive back the enemy?

_____
_____
_____
_____
_____
_____
_____
_____
_____
_____
_____

Question: What are some specific ways you can reflect the light of God to the world?

_____
_____
_____
_____
_____
_____
_____
_____
_____
_____
_____

Question: To what extent are you trusting in God's provision? Are you trying to provide for yourself apart from God? Where and how should you strengthen your trust in Him?

_____

_____

_____

_____

_____

_____

_____

_____

_____

_____

_____

_____

Question: What spiritual ground do you need to take? What possible plan or destiny has God equipped you for?

_____

_____

_____

_____

_____

_____

_____

_____

_____

_____

Action: Let your hope and faith in God propel you to capture spiritual ground—your identity, your hope, your life, your future. Help show others the way of freedom and hope. Every day, get dressed for success and victory in battle against your spiritual enemy, wearing the armor of God. When challenges rise up against you, take up the Word as your sword, reflect God's light as a beacon for the lost, and drive back the enemy! Equipped with His all-sufficient provision, be a child of hope and the light of the world.

Chapter 4 Notes

CONCLUSION

Truths of the Kingdom

We are children of the King! Let's humble our hearts, learn from God, and allow Him to strengthen our stance in the face of the enemy. The enemy's strategy is to hold you captive. Jesus comes to tell us that we are already free. Christ has swung the jail door wide open. Nothing can stop us from walking out, except our own crooked beliefs. There are three things we should keep in mind as children living in the Kingdom. Let's strive to bring these things from our heads to our hearts so that this knowledge resides within us.

Jesus is here to save, not condemn.

John recorded a conversation between Jesus and a man named Nicodemus. Nicodemus was struggling to grasp the ways of the Kingdom. Jesus told him, "For this is how God loved the world: He gave his one and only Son, so that everyone who believes in him will not perish but have eternal life. God sent his Son into the world not to judge the world, but to save the world through him" (John 3:16-17 NLT). Jesus saves!

The first thing you need to grab hold of as a Kingdom kid is the concept of security. If you think your salvation is based on what you do, you've misinterpreted the Good News. You lack trust in God's provision. The Good News says your salvation and your security in Christ is not based on your actions. The Good News is that God cares enough about you to give His life for you, even while you were lost in sin. He didn't come to condemn the world; He came to rescue the world, to salvage the world, to put the world back into a right relationship with the God of the universe. Understand that your hope is placed on solid ground. Your salvation is secure. Your creator has made a provision for you.

Don't try to earn what God freely gives. If you do, you will be tired and worn out, never accomplishing the great things God has created you to do. Religion tells us to act a certain way and to keep the law perfectly. Jesus says to simply trust. Once you do that, you will start becoming great in life.

We have to understand that our identities are based on Christ. He is the foundation to understanding ourselves and our purpose on Earth. Every single person on the planet—with no exception—is here as a result of two people coming together, under whatever circumstances that might be. We were all physically conceived and birthed by our mothers and fathers. You can't change who your birth parents are, even if you were raised by someone else. No matter what you do, they are still your parents. In the same way, if you've been birthed by your heavenly Father through your belief in His Son, then you can't change your identity as a child of God. He is your Father. Your identity is set. You are secure.

Some people don't embrace life because they've had a bad experience with an earthly father. The truth is that all of our fathers here on Earth may mess up. We're all sinners. A loving father can have a momentary lapse, and an unloving father is in no way representative of our heavenly Father. God will not abandon us. Our heavenly Father is not an earthly father. He is a Father who created you and gave His Son so that you could come to Him. He is not going to condemn you; He is going to embrace you. He's going to help you become all that you were created to be.

Your identity in Christ is simply recognizing who your Father is. What we think is what we become, and when that seed of thought is planted in your mind, it will change your actions. Recognize your good, loving, magnificent heavenly Father. Change your thinking and change your life. Jesus did not come to condemn. He came to save!

Jesus is not complicated.

Matthew records one of the prayers of Jesus: "O Father, Lord of heaven and earth, thank you for hiding these things from those who think themselves wise and clever, and for revealing them to the childlike. Yes, Father, it pleased you to do it this way!" (Matthew 11:25-26 NLT). He says that the Truth is revealed to the *childlike*. The minds of children are not complicated.

The minds of children cannot complicate God's simple truths.

Jesus continues in the same passage:

> Come to me, all of you who are weary and carry heavy burdens, and I will give you rest. Take my yoke upon you. Let me teach you, because I am humble and gentle at heart, and you will find rest for your souls. For my yoke is easy to bear, and the burden I give you is light. — **Matthew 11:28-30 NLT**

If you are tired and worn out from serving God, then you've probably overcomplicated the message of Jesus. He tells us that when we come to Him, we find rest for our souls. He teaches us how to walk and how to live. He tells us to follow Him instead of the world. In the world's system, it's hard for us to become like children because our inclination is to believe that there is retribution for wrongdoing. Our inclination is to do certain things to earn God's approval. But Jesus tells us to keep it simple. God is pleased with us because of what Jesus accomplished. That's it!

God is not confusing.

Scripture tells us that God is not the author of confusion (1 Corinthians 14:33). That doesn't mean that we have to understand every nuance of everything in the Bible. There may be things that our finite brains may never, ever figure out. However, the Bible is crystal clear from front to back that God loves all of us, that He sent

His Son into the world because people could not make themselves right with God, and that our salvation rests on the work of Jesus on the cross. The gospel is a simple message. Anything that causes confusion and disorder is not the work of God.

Why do we tend to obsess over minor details and miss the big picture? I've sat in seminary classes where people were discussing whether Adam had a bellybutton or not. Who cares? I don't know if he did or didn't. What I do know is that Jesus came from heaven to Earth. It is authenticated by the Word. It is authenticated by history and archeological evidence. He died on the cross, resurrected, and ascended into heaven. He resurrected because He wants our own lives to resurrect with Him. Understand what's important and don't linger on confusing details. Don't make a mountain out of a molehill! God is not confusing.

Paul teaches that the Church should not be confusing to people on Earth (1 Corinthians 14). The example of believers should not give the impression that we have to do specific things in order to be "spiritual." Paul says it's about the message—understanding who Jesus is and telling others who He is, so they can meet the King and become a Kingdom kid. The gospel is not complicated. Our lives should be testimonies drawing people into the Kingdom, not deterring them with obscure details and confusing tangents.

Rise Up in Hope!

We are children of the Kingdom. We have amazing potential. We can work together to bring light into the world. God has given us everything we need. He has given us the gift of life through Christ. He has given us a complete set of armor to put on every single day. He has given us a set of keys. He has given us His Word so that we can live out our purpose in life and shine the light of Jesus in our communities. Hope is here because Jesus has come! Embrace the hope of Christ because it will change your life.

The King is changing the world. He is bringing hope and healing into our cities. He has come for the confused, helpless, brokenhearted, and those living on the wrong side of the road—from the self-righteous side to the wayward. He reveals the truth both to the lost wanderers and the "religious." Jesus is building His Church. He gives them full access to all the Father's resources. He welcomes all into His loving embrace. He calls us to find others and usher them through the gates. You are part of the Church He is building. He is the chief cornerstone, the secure foundation. Knowing this, rise up in hope!

About the Author

Clay NeSmith is the Lead Pastor of Barefoot Church. He is a dynamic, high-energy speaker with a heart and a vision to reach the world. He is gifted in creating environments for people to discover all that God has created them to be. He is known for his ability to captivate his audience by delivering the Word of God in a way that is relevant to our world today.

Pastor Clay lives in South Carolina with his wife, Kim. They have one son, Cole, who is actively involved in ministry. The NeSmiths also have a dog, Ivan, who is dear to their heart.

About Sermon to Book

SermonToBook.com began with a simple belief: that sermons should be touching lives, *not* collecting dust. That's why we turn sermons into high-quality books that are accessible to people all over the globe.

Turning your sermon series into a book exposes more people to God's Word, better equips you for counseling, accelerates future sermon prep, adds credibility to your ministry, and even helps make ends meet during tight times.

John 21:25 tells us that the world itself couldn't contain the books that would be written about the work of Jesus Christ. Our mission is to try anyway. Because, in Heaven, there will no longer be a need for sermons or books. Our time is now.

If God so leads you, we'd love to work with you on your sermon or sermon series.

Visit www.sermontobook.com to learn more.

44455387R00073

Made in the USA
San Bernardino, CA
15 January 2017